RAINWATER HARVESTING FOR YOUR HOMESTEAD

A STEP BY STEP PLAN TO SAVE MONEY USING A CLEAN
AND SUSTAINABLE WATER SUPPLY FOR YOUR
GARDEN, LIVESTOCK, AND HOME

HAYDEN WARNER

CONTENTS

INTRODUCTION

We forget that the water cycle and the life cycle are one.

— JACQUES YVES COUSTEAU

You can live up to three weeks without food—but only three days without water. For homesteaders, securing a reliable water supply is one of their most prescient considerations. But how can you make sure your water supply is not only reliable, but clean, safe to drink, and renewable?

If you're a homesteader, you probably have a way to get water without relying on having rainwater lined up—at the very least, you should! Homesteaders are crafty people, as we're sure you know if you are one, and there's a wide range of ways to get water besides municipal hookup. You may have a well with a pump, or collect water from a nearby lake or stream. But what if your well runs dry, or if you lose access to the natural body you're drawing water from, or if it becomes contaminated? You need to have a backup way to get water.

It's not often you get a solution to your problems literally falling out of the sky! At the same time, there's more to collecting rainwater than just putting a barrel under your gutter and calling it a day. Not only do you have to make sure your rainwater is safe to drink, but you also need the right equipment if you want to collect enough water to sustain yourself and your family.

This book is for all those homesteaders who are interested in collecting rainwater. Whether you are just starting out, or if you want to learn a little more about securing a sustainable water source for your home, this guide will tell you everything you need to know. To start things off, we take a look at some of the benefits of rainwater harvesting, as well as why it's important for your family and your community that we all try to live as sustainably as possible. In Chapter 2, we discuss the legalities of rainwater harvesting and what you have to look out for if you're new to the practice in your area. If you've never had a rainwater harvesting system before, Chapter 3 tells you all about the most basic principles of permaculture, while Chapter 4 looks at ways in which rainwater can be collected using earthworks alone. Chapters 5 and 6 look at designing, sizing, and installing your very own rainwater harvesting system, while Chapters 7, 8, and 9 deal with possible problems, safety and maintenance considerations, and the treatment of water to make sure you and your family stay safe. Finally, Chapter 10 digs deeper into the different ways you can use your rainwater—and voila! Now you're one step closer to saving money and creating a clean and sustainable water supply for your home and garden!

CHAPTER 1: WHY HARVEST RAINWATER?

A s a resourceful homesteader, you probably don't want to let a resource that literally falls out of the sky go to waste. But what would you do with rainwater once you have harvested it, and why is all that effort worth it?

In the introduction, some reasons are introduced as to why you might want to harvest rainwater; for instance, you can use it to supplement your main water supply, or as a fallback in case something happens to the main supply. But in this first chapter, we're going to dig deeper. We'll go over what rainwater harvesting really means, what it can mean for your homestead, and the many things you can do with rainwater once you have it.

WHAT IS RAINWATER HARVESTING, REALLY?

If I were asked to explain rainwater harvesting in a nutshell, all I'd have to do is point to the rain rolling off someone's roof or sitting in puddles on the ground. All of that could have been collected and put to use. While many people don't think of the rain as something valuable, water is one of the most important requirements of life, second only to oxygen. When we don't have it, we certainly know it's missing. If you were ever in a situation where you didn't have access to your main water supply, having a backup stockpile of rainwater—and a way to get more—could be lifesaving, or more commonly, money-saving! As the common saying goes—waste not, want not.

Usually, rainwater harvesting uses a roof or another flat, slanted surface to direct rainwater into either irrigation channels, a container, or a pond. The broad surface area of a roof, for instance, collects much more water than a deeper bucket or barrel with a narrow opening would, and the slant uses gravity to direct the water where you want it to go. Other systems don't involve a roof at all, and simply shape the ground to direct rainfall into a garden or pond—see Chapter 4 for more on how this works. Harvesting systems can also include other components such as purification filters, and it all depends on what you want to use your rainwater for.

In this section, we're going to go through the actual reasons why harvesting rainwater can boost your homestead's productivity and potential, as well as the different ways in which it can be done.

Note: Henceforth, we'll be using the acronym RWH for "rainwater harvesting" to keep things simple and to avoid repetition.

The Benefits of Collecting Rainwater

Increasing Your Water Supply

First, and most importantly, harvested rainwater can supplement your main water supply. At the core of this benefit is what is discussed in the introduction: Every homesteader needs to think about where their water is coming from, because even the deepest well or biggest lake is not indestructible. RWH, therefore, is a way to get your hands on water that is, for the most part, completely independent of what's happening around you and is relatively unpolluted. Unless you're worrying about radioactive rain in the event of a nuclear catastrophe—which you probably aren't—there are far fewer ways rain could become completely unusable, especially in the foreseeable future. On the other hand, there are plenty of ways that your main water supply could become unavailable. For example, a river can become polluted by upstream dumping, a lake can be drained, or a shallow well can dry up.

On a less dramatic note, if something breaks in your primary water system—for example, if your electric well pump needs repairs—you can use your stored rainwater. In addition, you can also increase the amount of potable water you have available by substituting water that doesn't have to be pure or drinkable for rainwater. Using harvested rainwater to irrigate crops or flush your toilets, for example, saves a *lot* of water from your main water supply over time.

Helping the Environment

Moving and consuming water places a lot of strain on the environment, especially if you're hooked up to municipal water or have water otherwise transported to you. That is why there are so many environmental benefits to harvesting your own rainwater:

- Having an effective RWH system means that zero energy in the form of gas or electricity is used to bring water to your home.
- RWH prevents you from drawing water from rivers, lakes, or the ground, thus saving more water to be used later—even by future generations.
- Groundwater is being depleted in many regions, so harvesting rainwater will help reduce the burden on Earth's biggest supply of freshwater.

Easy Design, Construction, and Maintenance

Most homesteaders love their independence, so RWH fits right in with a self-sufficient philosophy. You won't have to rely on anyone else to harvest water for, or deliver water to you. In addition, with a little research, you won't have to call in a professional if something breaks. If you plan it well, it's possible for you to build and maintain a simple RWH system using materials you can find at any hardware store. A simple cost-benefit analysis will reveal that harvesting rainwater is well worth the relatively small amount of energy and money you need to put in.

Reducing Erosion and Flooding

Erosion and flooding is caused by heavy rains, and it can both do terrible damage to crops and buildings. This damage may lead to you having to redo hours or days of work, or even call in a professional for costly repairs:

- Flooding can destroy crops and therefore require you to buy food—which defeats the entire purpose of homesteading.
- Floodwater can carry pesticides and fertilizers to places you *don't* want them to be.
- Erosion can degrade and wash away the fertile top layer of the soil and make it unsuitable for growing crops.

If you live in a rainy area—like most people interested in RWH—you've probably taken measures to prevent your homestead from being damaged by flooding and erosion. RWH is another way to make sure that your homestead will be safe when it's really raining buckets. Not only does it collect water and direct it somewhere it can be useful, but an effective RWH system also works to slow down and spread out the flow of water so that when it hits the soil, it will infiltrate between particles instead of flooding on top or washing them away—see Chapter 3 for more on this.

A Small Upfront Investment

Above, we mentioned cost-benefit analysis in terms of time and energy, but here, we're talking about getting more bang for your buck—literally! Since anyone can build a simple RWH system with basic and readily available materials, you don't have to spend hundreds and hundreds of dollars—as long as you're willing to do some research and put in some elbow grease. As a further advantage, you'll probably also save money in the long run, as having a ready—and free—supply of water falling out of the sky saves a lot of resources.

The Many Different Uses of Rainwater

RWH isn't just for watering your garden, although that's one of its most popular uses, and it's not difficult to see why. Whether you've built something simple with a hammer and nails, or just did a few clever things with your landscaping, one of the best uses for harvested rainwater is crop irrigation. The good news is that if you intend to use your water in this way, you don't have to be stringent about purifying it, as plants aren't as picky about their drinking water as we are.

If you are willing to put a little more work into purifying the water—either in the RWH system itself or afterwards—you and your livestock can also safely drink rainwater. There are also many other ways in which rainwater can be used, and these are discussed later in the chapter.

RWH Methods

Most people think of RWH as something that's done by putting a barrel under your gutter, but there are many other and more efficient ways to collect rain and put it to good use. This section discusses several common methods of rainwater harvesting and gives a brief look into how each one is supposed to work, and what their various advantages and disadvantages are.

Rain Barrels

Rain barrels are cheap and require little effort in terms of installation and maintenance. Furthermore, you can get a rain barrel at any home improvement store, and you can even use any drums or barrels lying around at home, provided it's clean. However, even though it's a simple system, there are a few things you have to consider when installing a barrel:

- If you're using a secondhand or recycled barrel, you have to make sure that no harmful chemicals or dairy products have ever been stored in it. This is extremely important as harmful residue can get into your water. If you're buying a used barrel, ensure it's marked "food-grade" and that the salesperson can tell you what it was used for before.

- Your house, barn, or shed should be equipped with a gutter at the edge of the roof. Once this is in place, simply place the rain barrel under the spout in order to catch the rain falling out.
- You can install filters in the gutter to catch leaves and dirt.
- Purpose-made rain barrels come with a spigot at the bottom which you can attach your garden hose to.
- It's best to cover a rain barrel with a lid or screen when it's not raining to prevent debris from collecting in the barrel and mosquitoes from breeding in the standing water.
- Remove the rain barrel during winter/when the temperature is below freezing—letting the water freeze inside a barrel can cause it to crack.

The downside to rain barrels is that even if you put them under multiple gutters, you're not collecting as much rain as you could be. Furthermore, if you get a lot of heavy rain and your barrel fills up, you could become stuck with a full barrel that you'll have to move and replace once it overflows. This is not only a lot of work, but depending on the size of your barrel, it may even be impossible.

Dry Systems

The best alternative to a rain barrel is a dry system. With this type of RWH method, virtually everything is the same, except that instead of putting a barrel directly under the gutter, an additional structure is attached to the gutter to divert the flow of water into a much larger container—like a large water tank—located a few feet away from the building itself. Such a container won't be as cheap as a rain barrel, but it can also be purchased secondhand at affordable prices. Remember that if it has an open top, it should be covered to guard against mosquitoes, animals, and other debris and contaminants.

Wet Systems

If you're someone who lives in an area with a lot of rain, even a dry system might not be enough to harvest all the water you possibly can. In this case, a wet system consisting of an underground tank and collection pipes is your answer. A wet system works in a very specific way:

- The tank in this system is larger than one used in a dry system.
- Instead of being diverted from the end of a regular gutter, a different type of gutter is installed—or modified—so that water leaves it at multiple points; this reduces overflow in the gutter so you can harvest more water.

- When the water leaves the gutter, it moves down a series of pipes and enters the underground tank.
- You can draw water from your tank using a pump.

The downside of this system is that, while it collects much more water than the previous options, it is trickier and more time-consuming to maintain.

Green Roofs

What if you don't want to mess around with collection channels and containers, because all you want to harvest rainwater for is to irrigate crops? Consider building a green roof! A green roof is a series of garden beds installed on the roof itself. This system is great because it helps you make use of the rain with little effort. In addition, it also adds insulation to your home, protects the roof, and helps maximize your garden space. Green roofs have a few requirements:

- The roof has to be lined to prevent water or soil from leaking through into the rooms below.
- Choose low-maintenance plants so that you don't have to climb onto the roof every day, and so that rainwater will be enough irrigation for them. Hardy plants that can withstand full sun exposure are ideal.
- Ensure there is a route for excess rain to drain out of the beds to prevent puddles, leaks, flooding, or damage to the roof. You'll still need a gutter—you

could even place a rain barrel underneath it to double-up and catch overflow!

Earthworks Systems

You don't have to build a green roof to send rainwater straight to your crops. You can also create an earthworks system—in other words, you can shape the earth itself to trap rain and send it where you want it to go. There are many different types of earthworks systems to collect rainwater:

- A common component of an earthworks system is a barrier that will stop flowing water and either hold it or reroute it somewhere else, such as a dam. A variant of this is a barrage, which is a dam made out of wood, metal, or other materials, and that can be opened or closed.
- Earthworks systems can also include trenches, slopes, and other channels that direct water using gravity.
- Some of these systems funnel water straight into your garden, while others send it to a pond or other reservoir.
- Earthworks systems usually include some way of preventing water from seeping away into the ground —this is discussed in more detail later.

These systems can be simple or complex in nature—flip to Chapter 4 for more information!

Rain Saucers

If you're imagining a flying saucer, you're not far off—rain saucers are contraptions shaped like upside down UFOs, funnels, or umbrellas. These structures are made of metal or any other smooth material and are generally attached to a pipe to divert water to a container or tank. Their large surface area and sloped shape work to collect as much water as possible, and they are convenient because they don't rely on a roof—you can place them anywhere you want.

Water Collection Reservoirs

If none of the above options work for you, you can also consider installing a water collection reservoir. Essentially, this is a large concrete basin—such as a shallow pool— that is constructed to catch rain. These reservoirs are generally much, much wider than they are deep. The reason for this is that it maximizes efficiency, as something that is shallow but has a large surface area will collect more rain than something that is deep but has a narrow opening. Since water reservoirs are made of concrete, the water inside them isn't potable—but it's fine for irrigating your garden. Furthermore, if you're concerned about mosquitoes breeding in the still-standing water, remember that it doesn't have to stay in the reservoir. Instead, you can channel it into your garden or a storage tank using a barrage, trenches, water pipes, or other methods.

Didn't see anything here that jumped out at you? Or did you come up with an idea for a unique system tailored to your property and your needs? Don't worry—there is more information about designing and building a custom RWH system in Chapter 5.

So What's the Catch?

There are many reasons why we, as a society in the USA, don't use rainwater as our primary source of water. Although the country gets plenty of rain, there are some disadvantages to harvesting rainwater that may discourage homesteaders from relying on it too much.

The Rain Doesn't Follow a Schedule

RWH is much more popular as a key water source in regions of the world with a wet season and a dry season, where rainwater is collected in ponds or reservoirs during rainy periods, and then used to irrigate crops when it's dry. This system works well in these places because it's mostly possible to reliably say between which dates you can expect to get enough rain to fill your containers. Furthermore, RWH is also popular in places where better options aren't available.

While plenty of regions in the continental USA get rain year-round and/or have particularly rainy seasons, you can't predict for sure that you're going to get the kind of rain you're looking for at any given time. In addition, due to changes in the global climate, weather patterns are becoming even more unpredictable, and in many regions droughts and heatwaves are becoming more common. RWH therefore isn't a suitable primary method of collecting water for many homesteads, simply because it's not as reliable as a lake or well.

The Initial Investment

While the initial investment is small, there *is* an initial investment. It's true that you can save money by getting crafty with things you have at hand. However, the initial purchase of materials and setup may still set you back anything between $200-$2,000. That being said, depending on how much you spent and how productive your system is, it can pay for itself in 10-15 years.

Maintenance Concerns

You can't just "set it and forget it"—you need to continuously maintain your RWH system so that it stays efficient and that the water remains fit for consumption. Unfortunately, lots of wildlife—including rodents, roaches, lizards, and the ever-dreaded mosquitoes—are happy to live, breed, lay eggs, and die in standing water or damp places. It's therefore necessary to check your entire system regularly and clear out any uninvited guests. In addition, your tank or container also needs to be cleaned periodically to prevent algae and bacteria from growing.

Storage Limitations

No matter how efficient your system is, the truth is that you can only store so much rainwater. Even with an overflow system, your RWH system doesn't have infinite space. Therefore, once your tank is full, you won't be able to use your system until it's been emptied again; this is particularly problematic if you're saving up water to use for a specific purpose.

Contaminants From the Roof

Roofs are the basis of most RWH systems, because their broad surface area and sloped shape are perfect for catching and directing water where you want it to go. On the other hand, shingle and similar roofs can introduce animal droppings, lichen, bacteria, debris, and other contaminants into your RWH system. Thus, you should use a smooth metal roof—or something similar—to avoid this, or install a filter to purify your water. Alternatively, you can also clean your roof and gutters regularly, or use first flush diverters to avoid contaminating your water. This is discussed in more detail in Chapters 5 and 8.

Now that we've reached the end of this chapter, you've probably worked out *why* you want to start harvesting rainwater; maybe you've even gotten some ideas for what you could use it for—if you didn't have a plan already! Perhaps you've grabbed some scrap paper and started sketching out what your RWH system will look like... but don't get ahead of yourself! First, before you start designing your system, you need to make sure you're within your local laws and regulations. You don't want to build something up only to have to take it down later.

CHAPTER 2: TAKING CARE OF LEGALITIES

Most homesteaders—and even people in general—would agree that they shouldn't be banned from collecting a resource that falls out of the sky... but the fact of the matter is that in some regions, you might be. For a wide range of reasons, many states and municipalities have attached laws and restrictions to harvesting rainwater. If you want to start RWH on your homestead, it's imperative to be aware of these. You don't want to find yourself slapped with a nasty fine, or worse!

This chapter looks over the laws and legalities around RWH in the USA, why they exist, and how you can make sure you stay within the law. Just to give some context, we'll also discuss RWH laws throughout history, from ancient times up to the present day.

A LOOK AT THE HISTORY OF RWH

Historically, the practice of collecting rainwater is almost as old as humanity itself. From the very beginnings of our journey on this Earth, rainwater has been around to ensure human beings can stay alive. Without water, we cannot live: We have to consume it so that our bodies can function normally, and we also use it externally for hygiene purposes. In addition, we use water to sustain our crops without which we wouldn't have food—and therefore life. Water is often taken for granted, but the effects of not having access to any are often catastrophic and fatal. Droughts have caused immense suffering in many areas of the world, and it's one of the things we ought to be most afraid of. Thankfully, we have rainwater to keep us going—and if we learn to use our water more sustainably, we can ensure the longevity of our water sources and our species.

There are many historical accounts of different RWH technologies used by different societies, and it's therefore difficult to say with certainty where the practice originated from. However, it's believed rainwater was first harvested in 2000 B.C.E. by people living in the Negev Desert in the Middle East. Given the dry climate this civilization lived in, it was customary practice for them to capture water runoff from the hillsides and store it in tanks known as "cisterns." The rainwater was filtered by sediment traps before it entered the cisterns, and their storage capacity ranged from 10,000 to 50,000 gallons. One of the biggest cisterns was found in

Madaba, Jordan, and it was estimated it could hold up to 11,000,000 gallons of water at a time.

The practice of harvesting rainwater was also popular in ancient India. These civilizations developed advanced technology, some of which is still used today. For instance, stone gullies were built to feed rainwater into large vats that had been cut into the rock. In addition, RWH systems were also built on the top of the roofs of individual houses; this type of technology was later also used by communities in China and Brazil. Other components used to harvest rainwater in ancient India included *baoris*, which were wells that had been dug into the ground, storage tanks known as *jhalaras*, water storage dams that were referred to as *johads*, and *talibs*, which were reservoirs that contained the water typically used to drink or for irrigating crops.

The civilizations of ancient Rome are known for their innovative technology, some of which included RWH methods. The Romans designed entire cities around rainwater collection systems, which included gullies that diverted surface runoff from high-lying streets into cisterns, where the rainwater was stored. Some of these cisterns were enormous: For example, the underground Basilica Cistern in Istanbul can hold up to 2,800,000 cubic feet of water and contains 336 columns as part of its structure. It took 38 years to build using the labor of 7,000 slaves; today, it has become a popular tourist destination.

In ancient North America, Native Americans collected and stored rainwater that flowed off mountains to use for domestic and agricultural purposes. These systems contained trenches that were dug into the ground along the contours of mountain ridges and diverted rainwater into cisterns. Early settlers in the Americas were particularly fond of using rainwater to do their laundry because it didn't create "soap curd." They also collected rainwater in large barrels and used it for bathing.

It was a common practice to harvest rainwater in older societies, so why did people stop doing it? Over time, the cisterns used by ancient civilizations became increasingly contaminated. Because they had no way to remove the bacteria in the water, it spread diseases and made many people ill. Later, technology was developed that created the centralized water collection and purification systems most often used today. Since people no longer had a need for rainwater, they stopped collecting it. However, many farmers still continued to harvest rainwater to irrigate their crops and sustain their livestock.

Thankfully, RWH is once again becoming a trend in contemporary society, and many homesteaders are turning to the skies for answers to the question of using water sustainably. The technology used to treat water and remove bacteria has advanced tremendously since ancient times, and people once again feel safe using rainwater in their everyday lives.

RWH is important if we want to avoid running out of water entirely in the future. Societies and cities are growing rapidly, and our current way of obtaining water is depleting the natural water resources that exist underground. More people means more water, and we are using our ground-water at a faster rate than it is restored by rain. In addition, development in the form of roads, buildings, and stormwater drainage further decreases the amount of rainfall that can be taken up by underground water resources. Used water and storm water runoff is often directed into oceans and dams, and very little of it finds its way back into underground water tables. Our water sources are being reduced at a rapid and unsustainable rate, and if we don't start changing our ways soon, we may find ourselves in the middle of a terrible disaster.

In the USA, RWH is becoming more popular than ever, and many different states are trying to encourage people to make use of RWH systems. For instance, in some places people are offered rebates or tax incentives if they use RWH systems in their homesteads. As further encouragement, the American Rainwater Catchment Systems Association (ARCSA) was established to educate people on how to harvest rainwater and to motivate them to revive this ancient practice. This society also offers memberships to anyone across the globe who is interested in RWH, and they make a wealth of information available to their members.

RWH LEGISLATION IN THE USA

Installing a RWH system is costly and energy and time consuming, and it is important that you make sure you're legally allowed to do it before you make the necessary investment. In the USA, there is no nationwide legislation that specifically forbids or allows RWH, and it is up to individual states to make their own laws on this matter. For the most part, states either do not regulate RWH, or they try to encourage their citizens to harvest rainwater so that they can lighten the burden on the current infrastructure. It may seem absurd that people should be prevented from collecting a resource that falls from the sky and is free to all, but the truth is, RWH is illegal in some places. These laws are relatively unknown to most of us; that being said, it's necessary for people to know the reasons why they may be prevented from using rainwater in their everyday lives.

Generally, RWH laws have existed for many years and are the inheritance of a different time and way of thinking. In most places, RWH is not explicitly prohibited, but home-steaders may have to have permits to install these systems. Furthermore, the way these systems are built have to follow codes and regulations. Most often, RWH laws exist because it's difficult to decide whose water is whose, and how much each person is allowed to collect. Diverting water into your own collection system could take it away from someone else—such as your neighbor. For instance, the state of Colorado established a law 120 years ago that prohibits RWH because those who live upstream have an advantage over their downstream neighbors. Some laws therefore allow RWH, but restrict the amount of water that may be collected.

Another reason why RWH is regulated is because collecting rainwater reduces surface runoff, which could decrease the water levels of larger water bodies. In California, RWH was illegal until 2012 as a result of the possible disruption of natural ecosystems. Luckily for us, there are many places where RWH is legally permitted—in fact, 48 states allow rainwater to be harvested for domestic purposes. Even so, the way in which rainwater is harvested is still governed by certain regulations in some places. Some states have "limited regulations," which means rainwater can be collected legally, but certain rules have to be followed. In places with "state regulations," the requirements for RWH may be more strict, or it may be prohibited altogether. In addition to having regulations, certain states also offer incentives to encourage RWH. The table below will give you a better idea of the laws in each state, and what you are and aren't allowed to do as far as RWH on your homestead goes.

Name of State	Laws and Regulations
Alabama	There are no laws or regulations that prohibit or limit RWH.
Alaska	There are no laws or regulations that prohibit or limit RWH.
Arizona	There are no laws or regulations that prohibit or limit RWH, and there are county and city incentives for those who collect rainwater.
Arkansas	RWH systems are allowed, but they have to be designed by a professional, they have to adhere to the plumbing code, and they have to meet certain safety standards.
California	It's legal to harvest rainwater, but permits may be required in some instances, such as wanting to use rainwater indoors; however, a permit is not needed if the system is installed by a qualified professional. Some counties even offer tax rebates to those who make use of RWH technology.
Colorado	It's illegal to harvest rainwater, and individual households are only allowed to collect 110 gallons of rainwater in barrels, which may only be used for irrigation. At the same time, wells may be recharged using rainwater, so long as it's only collected from rooftops. Water from wells can also be used for indoor and outdoor purposes.
Connecticut	There are no laws or regulations that prohibit or limit RWH.
Delaware	There are no laws or regulations that prohibit or limit RWH.
Florida	There are no laws or regulations that prohibit or limit RWH.
Georgia	Harvested rainwater may only be used outdoors, and advanced systems have to be installed according to the standards outlined in the Plumbing Code. Tax incentives are provided for those who purchase and install RWH systems.

Hawaii	There are no laws or regulations that prohibit or limit RWH.
Idaho	While rainwater may be collected from rooftops and the ground, it cannot be collected once it has flowed into a natural waterway; homesteaders with RWH systems are also not allowed to infringe on anybody else's water rights.
Illinois	There are no laws or regulations that prohibit or limit RWH.
Indiana	There are no laws or regulations that prohibit or limit RWH.
Iowa	RWH became legal after the Plumbing License Law was amended in 2012.
Kansas	There are no laws or regulations that prohibit or limit RWH.
Kentucky	There are no laws or regulations that prohibit or limit RWH.
Louisiana	There are no laws or regulations that prohibit or limit RWH.
Maine	There are no laws or regulations that prohibit or limit RWH.
Maryland	There are no laws or regulations that prohibit or limit RWH.
Massachusetts	There are no laws or regulations that prohibit or limit RWH.
Michigan	There are no laws or regulations that prohibit or limit RWH.
Minnesota	There are a number of regulations that govern rainwater collection: RWH systems have to be approved by a qualified engineer, rainwater can only be used for non-potable purposes, and the quality of rainwater has to be monitored.
Mississippi	There are no laws or regulations that prohibit or limit RWH.

Missouri	There are no laws or regulations that prohibit or limit RWH.
Montana	There are no laws or regulations that prohibit or limit RWH.
Nebraska	There are no laws or regulations that prohibit or limit RWH.
Nevada	RWH became legal in 2017, but it's regulated and limited by certain codes: Rainwater may be used for domestic purposes that does not involve consumption, and it can also be collected and stored for wildlife.
New Hampshire	There are no laws or regulations that prohibit or limit RWH.
New Jersey	There are no laws or regulations that prohibit or limit RWH.
New Mexico	Permits are necessary for some RWH systems; in addition, harvested rainwater may only be used on site and exclusively for outdoor and domestic purposes, and the site's storm water runoff may not be affected by RWH efforts. At the same time, the state offers financial incentives for those who incorporate green building solutions—such as RWH systems—into their homes.
New York	There are no laws or regulations that prohibit or limit RWH.
North Carolina	As a result of the various water conservation efforts in the state, RWH is actively encouraged. Simultaneously, the Plumbing Code determines that rainwater can only be used for non-potable purposes, all pipes connected to RWH systems must be purple, and cisterns have to be marked with warning signs that the water contained in them is not safe to drink.
North Dakota	There are no laws or regulations that prohibit or limit RWH.

Ohio	While it is legal to harvest rainwater, it has to be done according to certain regulations set out by the Department of Health; these include what materials can be used in a RWH system, as well as how much water may be collected.
Oklahoma	The Water for 2060 Act outlines certain regulations regarding water use by homesteaders.
Oregon	Rainwater may only be harvested from rooftops, and RWH systems have to be placed outside; there may also be some areas where you will require a permit.
Pennsylvania	There are no laws or regulations that prohibit or limit RWH.
Rhode Island	There are no laws or regulations that prohibit or limit RWH.
South Carolina	There are no laws or regulations that prohibit or limit RWH.
South Dakota	There are no laws or regulations that prohibit or limit RWH.
Tennessee	RWH is encouraged by the state, and harvesting rainwater is a popular custom in this area.
Texas	RWH is encouraged through tax incentives, and those who purchase RWH systems do not have to pay sales tax for these systems. In addition, homeowner associations are not allowed to ban RWH systems, and homes with such systems may be exempted from a portion of their county property tax.
Utah	No more than 2,500 gallons of rainwater is allowed to be harvested, and a permit is required to do so; furthermore, collected rainwater has to be used on site.
Vermont	There are no laws or regulations that prohibit or limit RWH.
Virginia	RWH is allowed, but the water may only be used for non-potable purposes; in addition, rainwater may only be collected from roofs, and the first four inches of rainfall has to be diverted by a first flush diverter.

Washington	RWH is permitted, as long as the water intended for potable use was collected from a system that makes use of air gap fitting, and storage tanks containing non-potable water are marked appropriately. Furthermore, rainwater used for outdoor purposes can be collected from any surface, while potable water may only be collected from roofs; these two systems have to remain separate.
West Virginia	There are no laws or regulations that prohibit or limit RWH.
Wisconsin	There are no laws or regulations that prohibit or limit RWH.
Wyoming	There are no laws or regulations that prohibit or limit RWH.

Laws are ever-changing, but it's unlikely RWH will become illegal in the future because there are many financial and environmental benefits to collecting our own water. In addition, given the potential water crisis we're facing—and that has already made itself known in many parts of the world—we can't afford to let an opportunity such as this one pass us by.

Now, you've figured out whether or not your state regulates rainwater, as well as gotten familiar with any restrictions, why they exist, and how they're enforced. You've also learned a little about the history of RWH around the world. At last, it's the moment you've been waiting for—time to start looking into *how* to harvest rainwater, what your system will look like, and what you can hope to collect with the resources you have.

CHAPTER 3: THE EIGHT PRINCIPLES OF RWH

T his chapter isn't long—its purpose is just to give you a 101-level understanding of the eight key things you need to remember to perform RWH safely and effectively. These simple but essential principles are based on a mix of physics and math, and they will help you to design the best rainwater harvesting system you possibly can.

RWH IN EIGHT QUICK STEPS

The principles you're about to read about are derived from "permaculture," which is an ancient technique of developing sustainable and self-sufficient ecosystems, and that is once again becoming more cutting edge today. Permaculture covers a lot of topics—including land management, town planning, and creating self-renewing agricultural projects.

When designing a permaculture-based system, the key is to remember how things would work in the natural world. For example, in nature, electric pumps don't exist, and water flows according to the direction of gravity. So, if you wanted to create a system based on permaculture, you'd set it up so that water is always expected to flow *downwards*—just like it would in any wild river or stream.

Without further ado, here's a look into eight permaculture-based principles of RWH you can incorporate into your own homestead.

Watch How Things Work

In most guides, this step is called "Begin with long and thoughtful observation" (Lancaster, 2022). Before you build your RWH system, go outside while it's raining to the spot you're planning to build on, and watch how rain behaves when it falls on the roof, wall, and ground. Is water being "funneled" into a specific crack or niche in the structure? Which way does it naturally flow? When it rolls off the roof, where does it land on the ground? Also consider where does it seem like the runoff *doesn't* want to flow—is it being pushed away from a certain spot? Use this information to design a RWH system that flows as naturally as possible.

Work From Top to Bottom

To quote Lancaster (2022), "Start at the top of your watershed and work your way down." As mentioned in the intro to this chapter, you want to work *with* gravity, not *against* it. If you're building a RWH system on a roof, start designing at the highest point possible. Doing this will help you create a simplified system in which the water flows more naturally, and in which gravity is being used to your advantage. In addition, it will also minimize the amount of water entering your system at any given time.

If this sounds confusing, think of it this way: When you think of your system at the highest point of the roof, you only have to consider the rain that's falling there. On the other hand, if you start at the bottom, you have to take into account all the water that's falling at the entrance as well as all the rain that has flowed down from above this point. Remember that working with less water at the start may sound counter-intuitive, but it does let you spread out and

slow the flow of water more easily so it can properly infiltrate the soil in a permaculture system; this is discussed in
more detail later.

Start Simple

Rome wasn't built in a day, and a complex RWH system
shouldn't be either! The next principle of rainwater
harvesting is to "start small and simple" (Lancaster, 2022). In
other words, don't bite off more than you can chew by
building a complex system that is too much for you to maintain with the manpower you have—whether that's just yourself or the other people on your homestead too. Harvesting
some rainwater is better than harvesting none at all, and
building a basic system first lets you get a feel for the RWH
process and how much time, money, and effort you will have
to invest in the future to maintain your system. It also makes
it easier to figure out what the problem is if your first system
doesn't work the way you want it to. Building a RWH system
is a big investment, and it wastes much less time, energy, and
materials to start small now and build up later, than to start
with something big and complicated and then have to tear it
down.

Slow Down and Spread Out the Flow

As Lancaster (2022) says, "Slow down, spread out, and infiltrate the flow of water." The purpose of this principle lies
mainly in permaculture. If you're funneling your RWH
system into a garden, vegetable patch, or anywhere else

where water has to go into the soil, you don't want gallons of runoff hitting the ground with force at one time. Instead, you want the water to reach the ground slowly and over a wide surface area so it can sink into the soil and not flow over the top and be lost to the storm water system. Think about it: When you water a garden, you don't dump five gallon buckets of water on top of the plants all at once. Oh no—you're more likely to use a hose or watering can that spreads out the water and slows down its flow to prevent flooding. The same principle applies here in a RWH system.

Plan For Overflow

Not planning for overflow would be a bit of a shame—no homesteader likes letting a valuable resource go to waste!

Even if you think your area is too dry for the possibility of getting too much water, try to imagine where the water will go if the main path in your RWH system overflows. RWH guides tell you to "always plan an overflow route and manage overflow as a resource" (Lancaster, 2022). There are many ways to do this, and the specifics of your overflow system will depend on your unique setup. For instance, if your RWH system is mainly directed into your garden, you could create an overflow route by channeling water into a container that can be used to water the garden later.

Use the Groundcover

"Groundcover" refers to plants that spread out and cover the ground—like grass. A lot of people think of groundcover as purely ornamental, but these plants are important because their roots hold the soil together to prevent it from eroding. Additionally, groundcover also slows down the flow of water to prevent flooding. Another benefit of these covering plants is that they choke out weeds, attract pollinators, and help provide some shade to other plants from direct sunlight.

There are many ways to cover the ground in open spaces in your garden, as well as in vegetable patches and flowerbeds. For example, you can plant covering plants on uncovered soil, or you can plant smaller plants *inside* a vegetable garden around the very plants themselves. At the end of the day, the goal is to create a "living sponge" that can collect any excess water and prevent flooding by helping water that comes out of your RWH system to soak into the soil of your garden. Thus, when building a permaculture-style RWH system, you should seek to "maximize organic and living ground cover" (Lancaster, 2022).

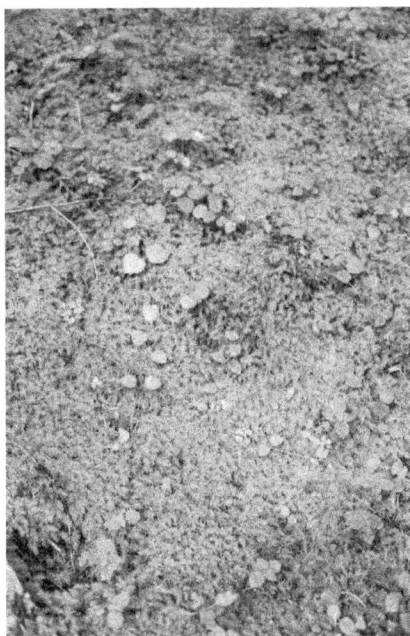

Have Your System Multi-Task

As we've mentioned above, a permaculture-style RWH system should imitate nature as closely as possible, and in nature, it's rare for any feature of the landscape to exist for more than one purpose. Therefore, "maximize beneficial relationships and efficiency by stacking functions" (Lancaster, 2022). In other words, build your RWH system so that if something can multitask, it should. An example would be to use dams to stabilize a footpath, which can simultaneously double as a berm to keep the water contained in your garden.

Back to the Start

A homesteader's work is never done! This is why it's important to continually assess your RWH system if you want to make it as effective as it can possibly be. Is there one part you're constantly fixing or getting annoyed by? Look at how you might be able to make the water flow a bit more naturally in this area, or how you can make your system more efficient by adjusting or replacing some of the components. Also consider how your garden is responding to the water you're directing into it, or how your household functions differently now that you're harvesting rainwater. Has your life become easier? Are you saving money? Is your garden flourishing, and is your family happy and healthy? Lancaster (2022) calls this the "feedback loop," and it's important to constantly reevaluate and adjust your system as necessary.

Now that you've learned these eight simple principles, you've probably gone back to the drawing board to start designing the RWH system of your dreams… we hate to stop you again, but you should know that creating a complex system to rig onto your gutter isn't the only effective way to harvest rainwater. Using the earth itself, you can create earthworks and landscaping systems to boost how much you harvest *before* you even head to the hardware store for pipes and barrels!

CHAPTER 4: EARTHWORKS AND SIMPLE LANDSCAPING

People have been shaping the earth around them for thousands of years: They built huts, houses, walls, roads, and fortifications out of earth. In addition, they have also used trenches, dams, and other earthworks to collect and direct rainwater.

Using the earth to divert water is a very ancient form of RWH that was invented long before human beings started making complex structures out of metal and plastic, and these systems are usually relatively simple when compared to contemporary forms of RWH. However, that doesn't mean you can just grab a shovel and get to it—knowledge and planning is necessary to create a working earthworks RWH system. Therefore, this chapter is dedicated to exploring what you can do with the earth to harness the rain and make it work for you.

DESIGNING AN EARTHWORKS RWH SYSTEM

Earthworks and other landscape implements are most commonly used to irrigate crops—either by directing rainfall through dedicated channels that lead directly into the garden itself, or by sending rainwater into a pond or reservoir to be stored until needed, such as during the dry season in arid climates. Therefore, as with any RWH system, you need to consider the space and materials you have available as well as the purpose you want this water to serve when building your earthworks system. There are different components to an earthworks system, and there are different ways to use these components—so before you get started, it's best to first get some background information about harvesting rainwater using the earth.

Where Will the Rain Fall—and Where Will It Go Afterwards?

The first thing to consider is how much rainfall you're planning for: Are you expecting massive seasonal monsoons, or year-round showers, or something in between? While every good RWH system has something in place for any overflow, you want your earthworks system to be the right size to handle the rainfall you're expecting.

In the world of RWH and earthworks, "rainfall" is defined as any water that falls off another surface—be it out of the sky, off a roof, a purpose-made structure, or the branches of a tree (Waterfall, 2004). When it comes to considering rainfall, it's not only the volume of water you have to consider—rainfall duration is just as important; for instance, an hour's heavy rain will behave differently than a day's light drizzle, even if the overall amount is the same.

In addition to considering the rainfall, you also have to think of vegetation. Remember that the plants you select for your garden must be suited for the type of rain you expect to get. Some plants are relatively hardy and can deal with changes in irrigation, such as the volume of water they receive, or when they receive it. Others are more sensitive—they may either need a lot of water at frequent intervals to thrive, or they may be delicate and used to dry climates, and therefore prone to drowning. The easiest way to select the right plants for your earthworks system is to choose vegetation that is native to the region you live in, because this will ensure they're well suited to the amount of rain you're going to get throughout the year. As well as selecting the right plants, the earthworks system itself should be built in such a way that it can channel water in a way that'll allow your plants to thrive.

But how do we make sure that the earthworks system is suited to the plants you're growing? One thing to consider is where the rain will fall: Will it be on an impervious surface—like wood, metal, stone, or very densely packed dirt—that it cannot seep through and infiltrate, or will it be on a permeable surface where the water will easily sink between earth particles, such as soil, regular earth, grass, or sand? This is important because in the first case, the water will "run off" immediately and then go somewhere else, while in the second case, the water will be soaked into the surface like a sponge, and it will only run off once the "sponge" is completely saturated. You can use this difference in the water's behavior to direct rainfall where you want it to go; for example, you can create a living sponge out of edible ground cover to keep water in one place, or use impervious materials to send water down a channel instead of letting it sink into the ground.

COMPONENTS OF A SIMPLE EARTHWORKS RWH SYSTEM

In this section, we talk about some common structures that are found in earthworks RWH systems, as well as what each is typically made of, and for what purpose they're used.

Catchment and Distribution

When rain falls out of the sky, the first place it lands in your RWH system—whether it be a traditional system or an earthworks system—is the catchment area. As the name suggests, this is the area or structure that catches the rain. Ideally, your catchment area should be placed at the highest point of the RWH system—as discussed in Chapter 3—and it should have as large a surface area as possible. Remember, rainfall is spread out more or less evenly, so a broad, shallow catchment area will catch more rain than a deep, narrow one.

Even if the rest of your RWH system is earthworks, that doesn't mean your catchment area has to be. You can use your roof as a starting point, just as you would in most other RWH system designs. In this case, the rain can run down the roof and pour out of the downspouts, after which it can be pulled into the rest of the system by gravity. This is a very simple system to put in place, and therefore many people find this very convenient. If you don't want to use your roof as a catchment area, you can also use a rain saucer, a natural slope covered in rocks or tightly packed dirt, or a structure that you built to the right size and shape. No matter what you use as a catchment area, it's important that it's slanted so that it can direct the water in one direction by force of gravity. This will ensure it flows into the distribution system.

In addition to a catchment area, your RWH system must also have a "distribution system." In essence, this is the "road" your water is going to follow to its destination. There are a number of structures that can be included, but swales, trenches, channels, ditches, or similar dug-out paths are most commonly used. These should be reinforced with living sponges—as mentioned in Chapter 1—to protect them against soil erosion. They can also be lined with rocks for the same reason. Your trenches and channels should be deep enough to accommodate the amount of water you're expecting. At the same time, if you're worried about soil erosion in the case of overflow, you can build "berms"—low walls of soil or stone—on either side to provide a double layer of protection. If you want to control the speed and direction of the flowing water, you can build dams and gabions; just remember that you should always use gravity to your advantage. Make sure you're building with the assumption that water will flow downhill, and adapt your design to the slope of your property.

Other possible components you can incorporate into the design of your earthworks distribution system include natural rock formations, slopes, and hills. You can also build walls or curbs with cutouts to let water flow through, or dams, barrages, and gabions, to manage the speed at which water flows.

Dams and Barrages

We've already touched on these, but as they're a core component of many earthworks systems, it's important to mention them again. Dams are walls you build perpendicular to the flow of water—in other words, at a 90 degree angle, like a T. The purpose of a dam is to block the flow of water in a certain direction to a greater or lesser degree. There are several reasons you'd want to do this: You may want to stop the water from overflowing out of the side of the trench, gully, or channel, or you might want to force it to take a turn. You can also use dams to hold water in a reservoir or pond, or to protect the earth on the other side of the dam against soil erosion. Dams can be made of tightly packed dirt or clay —as they have been for thousands of years! Other possible materials include wood—ideally planks placed flush against each other—or stone masonry that fits together well.

A barrage is a type of dam that includes a gate that you can open or close to let water through or keep it in one place. If you're using a basin as a holding area for water before letting it flow into your garden or other channel, a barrage or gate inserted into the side of the holding area can be used to control when you let the water out.

Gabions

If you're not familiar with earthworks and permaculture, it's entirely possible this is a completely unfamiliar word to you! A "gabion" is like a dam that is intentionally left permeable— or "leaky"—so that some water can get through. Like dams, gabions are also placed perpendicular to the flow of the water. Their purpose is to slow down the flow of water and to allow it to spread out, in accordance with the principles discussed in Chapter 3. When gabions are made out of brush

—such as cut trees, branches, and bushes—they are called "brush dams" or "brush gabions." They can also be made out of rocks that are stacked in such a way that gaps are left for water to trickle through.

Because gabions slow down and spread out the flow of water, using them will prevent your plants from being drowned in oversaturated soil. It will also help water to properly infiltrate the soil instead of letting it rush through unhindered. Slowing water with a gabion also prevents soil erosion in areas where you don't want to lose a fertile layer of soil, or where you want to keep the ground structured the way you have it—you don't want a carefully-built system to degrade any faster than it needs to! Gabions can also be placed in sequence after a dam to slow down water that gets through, or they can be designed to break in order to slow down floodwater. When they are used for this purpose, they can be compared to a "pressure relief valve" that would prevent erosion by temporarily interrupting and slowing water (Castaldo, Parsons, and Ott Fant, 2021). Another useful aspect of gabions is that they give any plant matter or materials you had to clear for building that isn't suitable to be used for anything else a brand-new purpose. For instance, leafy branches and similar debris that might have been thrown out otherwise can be put to work in your RWH system as gabions.

An ideal gabion is low in height, usually only as tall as the depth of the channel. While many possible structures exist, the most common design is a row of vertical stakes driven into the bottom of a trench, channel, or gully, and across the site where you're building the gabion. If you're using branches, they can be woven through the stakes and secured to either side of the trench to give the appearance of a fence. It's best to set up two of these with a small amount of space between them; this space should be a couple of feet wide. To complete your gabion, you can fill it with more interwoven branches, as well as brush, rocks, dirt, or any other permeable material. If you want to use your gabion as a pressure valve for floodwater, this is the best type of structure to build because it will slow down small to moderate flows of rainwater and spread them out to reduce erosion and boost soil filtration. These types of gabions are also efficient in situations where the water pressure is mild and you need to quickly reconstruct the gabion if needed.

A more durable gabion option—which is ideal if your area gets heavy monsoons, or if you're expecting heavy or frequent flows of water—is rocks stacked in front of wire netting, which you can buy ready-made or make yourself. The metal as well as the rocks should be secured to stop them from falling apart under water pressure. If you don't want to use metal wire or netting, you can also stack big, heavy rocks on top of each other. Rock gabions are harder to knock down and take much longer to rebuild, but they also last longer. The option you'll choose will depend on your needs—there is more information about this in Chapter 5.

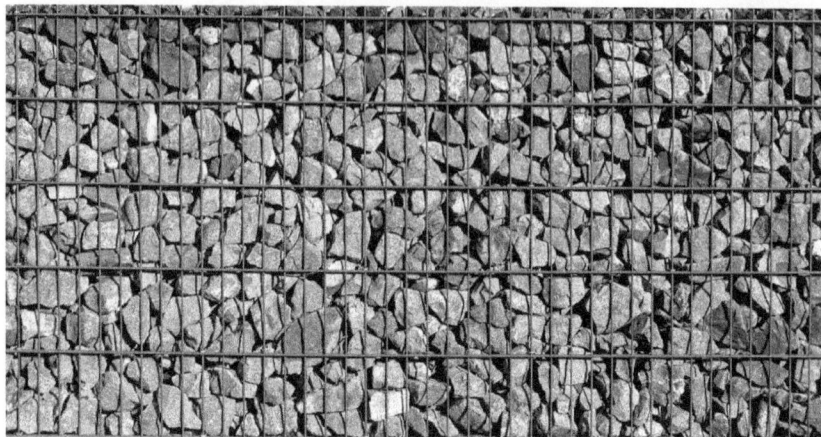

Pay attention to what the sides of your trench, channel, or gully are made of when planning your gabion. If it isn't strong bedrock—in other words, if it's made of soft soil that will erode easily—you need to build an "apron" for the gabion. This is a layer of rocks—ideally flat ones, but you can use what you have—that covers the bottom and sides of the channel or gully on the downstream side of the gabion. These guard against soil erosion from overflow during a storm, and they'll direct the water where you want it to go. A minimum-sized apron should be 1.75 times as long as the height of the gabion, but you can build it along the entire downstream length of the channel if that suits your needs better. The easiest way to construct an apron is to use rocks that are heavy enough to stay in place and not wash away, and to secure them with metal wire netting. You can also drive them into the ground itself. Don't forget to reinforce the sides of your trench, channel, or gully with a living sponge, as discussed in Chapter 1. This will help spread water out and make use of the water seeping into the earth; it'll also cut back on erosion. Always remember to inspect your gabions and aprons regularly to make sure everything is still in place, and update the design if you see that rocks and branches in your structure are being moved around by the water.

Landscape Holding Area

Your water has to go somewhere once it enters your RWH system, and in many systems, it's a "landscape holding area." This is a depressed or concave area of ground that water is intended to filter into, and that is lined with a thick layer of plants. These plants will help cut down on soil erosion and prevent flooding. Furthermore, if you use edible crops or trees that provide shade, they can also be multi-functional. It's important to choose the right plants so that they're suited to the amount of rainfall they'll receive—see the beginning of the chapter for more on plant selection—and the easiest way to get this right is to choose plants native to your area.

As mentioned above, a landscape holding area is typically concave, like a shallow bowl. While the right depression may occur naturally, it's possible you might have to dig one. If you want to make sure the water doesn't get away in case of overflow, you can build a low berm using the dirt and rocks you remove from the holding area, or any other materials you have on hand. If you don't want to dig out the entire landscape holding area, you can use a flat patch of ground in an appropriate place. If you do this, make sure that the plants are densely planted, and that the berm is higher. If you want to create a system to irrigate a range of crops that need different amounts of water, you can place two or more holding areas in sequence so all the water flows into the first, after which the excess will flow into the second, and so on. A crescent or semicircular berm, wall, or dam can be placed on the downhill side of your holding area to prevent overflow from getting out and damaging anything that doesn't need to be irrigated.

Basins

When someone says "basin," you probably think of a bathtub or sink, and the word means something similar in earthworks: A basin is a pond, reservoir, or other "container" that water flows into. Like everything else in this kind of system, basins can be lined and reinforced with berms or living sponges to reduce overflow and erosion. The basin can be used as a storage area for water you're later going to let out via a gate or barrage, a backup container for overflow, or even the water's final destination, for example, in the case of a duck pond. Dams, barrages, and gabions can be used to control when, how much, and how fast water flows into the basin, and like landscape holding areas, basins can also be placed in sequence.

Spillways

A spillway is a common overflow contingency in earthworks RWH systems. Essentially, it's a channel that allows excess water to leave the system in a slow, spread out, controlled way that doesn't erode the soil or flood your property. The idea is to use a dam, barrage, or other barrier to block off the entrance to the spillway, which should only be breached during a flood or overflow situation. In other words, a spillway only comes into play once the water level gets high enough to flow over its top. The spillway itself can have gabions or other permeable structures placed in sequence along it to slow and spread out the flow of water until all of it has been dissipated into the soil. As always, don't forget to include a living sponge! Finally, make sure all spillways are heavily reinforced by rocks and dense vegetation to prevent erosion and to stabilize the structure.

SWALES AND TERRACES, AND HOW TO BUILD THEM

Swales and terraces are structures that can be a bit more involved, but are useful enough to a simple earthworks RWH system—especially those constructed according to perma-culture-based principles—that we decided to give you more detail about how to set them up in your own system after explaining what they are and what they do!

Swales

A swale is essentially a channel that is wider than it is tall, with sides that gently slope downwards to allow water to enter from all directions. These are sometimes used to gather polluted water, but in earthworks, they can be placed along the edge of a basin or landscape holding area to collect runoff and overflow, slow it down, and to ultimately absorb it and prevent soil erosion. You can also use swales to collect overflow at any point along the RWH system and to hold it until it infiltrates the soil and is absorbed.

The bottom of the swale can be lined with mulch or covered with a thick layer of plants; these will act as a living sponge and protect the soil. If you decide to line the bottom of your swale with plants, remember that plant choice here is even more important than normal, since a swale is a protective structure. In addition to absorbing rainwater runoff, these plants can also be edible crops that you're trying to irrigate.

Before building a swale, look into the area around your RWH system, especially the final landscape holding area or basin. If you've already built the rest of your system, you already know in which direction water flows and where unwanted runoff builds up, and you can use this information to decide on the position of your swales. However, if you haven't done so yet, it is best to follow the natural slope of the ground. Furthermore, the swale should be at the lowest point of your garden or landscape holding area. When deciding on the location of your swales, there are a few other things you should keep in mind:

- The swale needs to be at least 10 feet from all buildings and 18 feet from any septic leach fields, hillsides, or steep slopes; this is because the swale cannot interfere with anything.

- The swale, the berm, and the plants reinforcing them must be able to actually absorb the water flowing in. This is not only so that you don't lose precious water, but also to avoid a landslide if too much water runs over a steep slope with a lot of loose soil, which can erode the slope and destabilize the ground.
- There needs to be a gentle slope preceding the swale with an incline that is no more than 25%, so that water can be pulled into the swale by gravity. In fact, ideally this incline should be even less than that (Castaldo and Ott Fant, 2019).

Once you know where the swale needs to be located, there are several steps you have to follow to construct the swale:

1. Determine and mark the contour line using an A-frame level. The contour line is the curve of the slope you're working with, and the contour you've marked should be the same elevation at all points. Making sure your swale is built level—*not sloped*—along the contour will guarantee the water is distributed evenly over the area inside, instead of being concentrated at the lowest point of the swale.

2. Once you have a marked contour line you're happy with, start digging a trench along the markings. An ideal trench has specific dimensions:

- The swale should be between half a foot to a foot and a half in depth, and its width should always be wider than its depth.
- For the purpose of a home garden, you probably don't have to make it wider than two feet. As for its length, you can make it as long as it needs to be.

3. A berm can be made by piling dirt on the other side of the swale while you dig. Typically, a berm has to meet several requirements:

- It needs to be thick enough to hold back flood water. Furthermore, a thick berm with a gradual slope will ensure the structure remains stable. An ideal berm is at least four times as thick as the height of the swale (measured from its bottom to the top of the berm). If there is not enough material in the swale itself, you may need to add more to make sure your berm is thick enough.
- The height of the berm will vary according to the depth of the swale, but should be about a third as tall as it is wide. The height of the berm is measured from the ground level to its top, and doesn't include the depth of the swale.
- Make the berm thicker if your soil is really loose and sandy, or if you live in an area with gophers or other burrowing animals.

- The berms should be compact enough to retain water, but the soil at the bottom of the swale should be left loose to let water infiltrate it.

4. Once you have dug the trench, take up the A-frame level again and walk through the bottom of the swale to ensure it is even all along its length; adjust it if necessary.

5. When your trench and berm is in place, you can start planting your living sponge. The specifics of your sponge should be determined by several factors:

- If you live in a dry climate, you can put plants inside the swale. However, if you're expecting a lot of water to fill it—for instance, enough to drown most plants —you should cover the berm with plants. If your area is very wet, you can even plant uphill of the swale trench itself, so that plants start slowing the flow of the water before it has reached either the berm or the swale.
- You can leave a strip of land unplanted between the trench and the berm and allow wild native plants to grow here, or even do the same with "walls" dividing the swale into sections.
- Hardy perennials that are suited to your area and that won't be harmed by some extra water are best. If the soil isn't fertile enough, use compost as needed.
- Use layers of mulch to absorb water anywhere you aren't planting a dense layer of vegetation.

- If you're not planting anything inside the swale, you can cover its inside with pebbles or rocks. This will help slow down the water as it enters the swale and help it infiltrate the ground. These pebbles and rocks can also be piled along the length of the swale to create gabions, which will slow down the horizontal spread of water.
- Don't be afraid to beautify the swale by giving the berm a rock border, planting ground cover over exposed soil, or anything else you can think of that doesn't interfere with the swale's performance. A swale doesn't have to be purely functional—it can easily become a feature in your garden!

6. You should plan for overflow in the swale—even if the swale itself is there to help prevent overflow:

- Spillways are a good idea here, as they can be used to direct the water into the soil, into another garden/landscape holding area, and even into *another* swale.
- Make sure the spillway is at least twice as wide as the height between the top of the berm and the bottom of the swale.

Terraces and Check Log Terraces

You've probably noticed—especially in our section on swales —that while hills and slopes are essential for an earthworks

RWH system, they can also pose difficulties. Rainwater that flows over steep slopes can cause erosion, destabilize your hard work, remove nutrients from the soil, and even lead to landslides. They can also make it difficult for swales to handle runoff, or even make it completely impossible. So what's a homesteader to do with a property covered in tons of steep slopes, hills, and banks?

A "terrace"—in the context of permaculture and earthworks —is a series of banks or platforms cut into the side of a steep slope. Their purpose is to reduce erosion by slowing down the flow of water, and to allow gardens to be planted and other earthworks structures to be built. Terraces have been used in agriculture and permaculture for thousands of years, and in that time, plenty of different types were developed.

One of the most popular types of terrace is a "check log terrace," in which each platform bank of the terrace is reinforced with stacked logs, sticks, and earth—almost like a fence or a beaver dam. This helps stabilize the structure and can provide a place to attach scaffolding if you're planning to grow climbing plants. Terracing a hillside with check logs will also ensure that the soil does not end up barren, because it'll help keep it aerated, stop the rain from carrying away fertile soil, and attract beneficial organisms. All of this will work together to let plants and vegetation grow freely to further stabilize the structure. In addition, check log terraces also help increase the fertility of your soil over time, as nitrogen-fixing plants and microbes—as well as worms and other useful critters—will be able to thrive without being washed away!

Building your own terrace is fairly simple—here are a few steps you can follow:

1. Using an A-frame, start by finding level contour lines. You want every level of the terrace to be flat and even to prevent water from collecting in one section; this is also the time to figure out how many levels your terraced slope will have.
2. Mark the contour line of each planned level.
3. Hammer stakes—ideally ones that are two inches wide, two inches thick, and thirty-six inches tall—into the ground every two to six feet along each line you've marked. Your stakes don't have to be expensive—if you have strong scrap wood, you can use that, or you can get them from most hardware stores at a fairly low price.
4. Layer cardboard sheets on top of the patch of ground behind the stakes—these will form the level part of your terrace. Lining the terraces with cardboard will kill off unwanted plants that could get in the way of your gardening. Make sure the cardboard pieces overlap and that zero light is getting through them.
5. Next, start building your beaver dam! Layer logs, branches, and sticks on top of your cardboard and behind the stakes to form a wall.

6. If the logs and branches you've decided to use are more than six inches in diameter, dig into the ground a little to give them a slot to rest in—this will ensure the stakes aren't straining to hold them back.

Including earthworks in your RWH system is very useful and it can make your lifestyle a lot more sustainable. However, if you want to take it a step further, you can incorporate other elements—such as storage tanks, pipes, and pumps—into your homestead. If this sounds like you, flip over to the next chapter and grab a notebook—it's time to start designing your RWH system!

CHAPTER 5: DESIGNING FOR YOUR NEEDS

Not every RWH system is designed to feed water directly into a garden. There are plenty of reasons to collect rainwater, and you need to take these reasons into consideration if you want the system to serve your needs. In this section, we take a look at the essential components of any working RWH system, as well as why you need them, and how they build on the principles we discuss in Chapter 3. We also look at how you can get started with the harvesting process—for instance, selecting the right size storage tank, the right pumps, and the right filters to get the job done. Finally, we briefly touch on the most important things you need to know about more intricate systems, and why it may be beneficial to you to eventually make your own system more complex; we also consider things you need to take into account to make sure your complex system will continue to work efficiently.

THE ESSENTIAL COMPONENTS OF EVERY RWH SYSTEM

A RWH system is made up of many different components, and the specifics of these will depend on your unique needs. However, there are certain parts that no system can function without—and before you begin designing your own system, you have to know what they are!

A Collection Area

The collection area of a domestic RWH system will most typically be the roof of your house. While it's possible to collect the water as it falls into your rain barrel, it is far more effective to harvest rainwater from a roof because its surface area is much larger. The collection area, or "catchment area," is the first place where the rain will fall. The material that your roof is made of will therefore have an enormous impact on the quality of your water, as will any debris or other things that are on your roof.

Other possible collection areas include paved areas—such as courtyards and terraces—lawns, and any other open ground. Swales are also considered catchment areas, even though the water collected in them is generally not directed into a storage tank.

If your catchment area is a roof—as it is in most cases—there are a few things you have to take into consideration when designing your RWH system:

▶ The material that the roof is made of will have an impact on how easily contaminants can be removed from its surface. A metal roof is the easiest to clean, and is therefore ideal if you're starting from scratch, while wood shingle roofs have a higher risk of contaminating water. In addition, the material itself can also serve as a contaminant. It's therefore best to avoid any metal that contains lead or harmful materials, such as asbestos. There are many possible materials to consider when building a catchment area:

- Tin is considered an ideal roofing material when it comes to RWH, because it has a low water loss rate of no more than 5%. Furthermore, provided it's been coated appropriately, there are no contaminants that can leach out of the tin into your rainwater.

- While asphalt shingles can work well in RWH systems, certain types can leach contaminants into your rainwater. In order to avoid this, it's best to consult with a professional before you choose a roofing material. In addition, shingles also have a water loss rate of between 8% and 10%.
- Wood, cedar, and shake shingles can only be used in RWH systems where the water is for irrigation only because they leach contaminants into rainwater. In addition, these materials also become moldy and promote algae growth, and this makes any water harvested from these roofs unsafe to drink.
- Clay tiles have a water loss rate of about 8%, but they don't contain harmful chemicals and generally work well in RWH systems.
- Ceramic, cement, and rubber roofs are all efficient RWH system materials.

▶ Be careful when coating your roof, as certain chemicals can make your rainwater unusable; for instance, biocides, fungicides, and algaecides should all be avoided if you want to use your roof as a collection area.

▶ The steepness of the roof will determine the rate at which water will run off it, which will in turn influence how easily water can become contaminated. A steep roof can be cleaned more easily as runoff will leave the roof surface faster. At the same time, a roof with a more gradual slope has a higher potential to remain contaminated after the runoff has left its surface. In addition, if your roof has a very gradual slope, you can also lose water to evaporation—especially if the rainfall is very light.

▶ The size of the roof will determine how much water can be collected. To determine the size of the roof, you have to find its "footprint:" Calculate the area of the building and add the area of the roof's overhang. The slope of the roof does not influence its footprint; these calculations are discussed in more depth in Chapter 5B.

▶ The shape of the roof will have an influence on the design of the conveyance system. Generally, most roof shapes work well in RWH systems. However, if the roof is also used as a deck, the contamination caused by foot traffic and the presence of human beings may make it unsuitable for RWH.

A Conveyance System

Once rain has fallen in the catchment area, it will have to be transported to a storage tank—and this is where your conveyance system comes in. This component refers to the various pipes and conduits—such as gutters and downspouts —that move water from one area to another. These pipes are typically made up of PVC, seamless aluminum, vinyl, and galvanized steel. Like your roof, the material you choose for the design of your RWH system is important. because it will influence the quality of your water. For instance lead cannot be used in potable water systems, as its toxicity can contaminate your water. In addition, your material choice will also determine the longevity of your system, as well as the amount of maintenance it will require.

Alongside the material, the design of your conveyance system is also important. When you start creating it, think of how you will clean the pipes, what gradient they have to be placed at, and how you can avoid blockages in them. You also have to think about how these pipes will be fastened— by using brackets or straps, for instance—and what they will be fastened to. Keep in mind that the weight of these components will increase dramatically once they have been filled with water. When this happens, you don't want gutters and downspouts sagging, coming loose, or falling out of place as this will reduce the efficiency of your RWH system, waste your time, energy, and money, and even endanger your family. Other questions you can ask yourself when designing your conveyance system are:

- How many tanks are there in your RWH system, how big are they, and where are they located?
- Are these tanks underground, aboveground, or a combination of both?
- Are there any local regulations that determine where rainwater tanks can and can't be placed on a property, and how does this impact the gutters and downspouts?
- Are you working with an existing structure, or do you have to design everything from scratch?

- If there is a structure in place already, what components does it have, and how can those be incorporated into the RWH system?

There are three key things that have to be considered when it comes to conveyance systems:

▶ The size of your gutters and downspouts will determine the efficiency of your overall system, and you have to make sure they are sized according to a 100-year storm event. Generally, gutters should be a minimum width of five inches. As for your downspouts, you must have one square inch of downspout for every 100 square feet of the area of your roof —these calculations are discussed in more detail in Chapter 5B. When sizing your conveyance system, remember that bigger isn't always better: Even a slight increase in the size of your pipes can dramatically raise the cost of your system, so make sure you calculate these sizes as accurately as possible.

▶ The installation of gutters and downspouts will determine if they're efficient and safe:

- For good drainage, gutters should be placed at a slope of a quarter inch for every 10 feet of gutter length you have (Bussey, 2022).
- Underground pipes have to have a minimum recommended slope of 2.08%.

- Gutters should be fastened with hangers at three foot intervals, or one foot intervals in places that receive heavy snowfall.
- To avoid water splashing against the building, you can place the front end of the gutter half an inch lower than the back.
- It's best to paint PVC pipes to protect them from the sun.
- Generally, rounded gutters are considered a better option, because they have less debris buildup in them than square or rectangular gutters.

▶ Gutters aren't uncommon, and we've become so used to seeing them that we rarely think of their aesthetic value. However, if you're worried about the pipes in your system being unsightly, you can paint them the same color as the building. Additionally, there are also many interesting designs and unique transition fittings that can make your conveyance system more pleasant to look at. Even though RWH is serious, there are many ways to have fun with it!

A Storage Tank

Possibly the most well-known component of any RWH system, a storage tank, cistern, barrel, or pond is essential—without it, you'll have no place to store your water! There is an endless array of storage tanks available in a variety of shapes—including round, rectangular, or square—and sizes, and the type you choose will depend on the climate you live in, the space you have available to you, how you intend to use your water, and how much rainwater you want to collect. This decision can also be influenced by the RWH legislation in your area, as discussed in Chapter 2. Different tanks come with different fittings—such as pre-tank filters, calmed inlets, overflow units, and spigots of different sizes— and the tank you choose will once again depend on your needs, and possibly your budget. These additional components can also be installed by yourself, should you have a tank that doesn't include something your system desperately needs.

You can choose whether you want to install your tank above ground or below ground, and this decision will depend on your specific needs. Each has certain advantages and disadvantages; for instance, underground tanks are better insulated against temperatures and are therefore less likely to freeze over. In addition, they're also out of the way, and they don't take up as much space as their aboveground counterparts. On the other hand, these tanks are more expensive to install and maintain. They can't be accessed easily, and therefore inspecting, repairing, and cleaning them can be difficult —and even costly. They can also crack easily because they're in constant contact with shifting and settling soil. In addition, the water stored in underground tanks can become polluted more easily by surface runoff if their openings aren't sealed properly. An underground tank will also require a pump to remove water from it.

For their part, aboveground tanks also have their disadvantages: They are permanently subjected to changing weather conditions, and extreme temperatures can damage your tank and contaminate your water. They also take up precious space—especially in urban environments where space is limited—and some may consider them aesthetically unpleasant. At the same time, aboveground tanks are cheaper to install and easier to maintain and inspect. Additionally, they can also be used with a gravity-fed conveyance system, which means you won't have to worry about water pumps.

As for materials, storage tanks are typically made from plastic or galvanized steel, but they can also be constructed out of other materials, such as concrete or fiberglass. Your choice of material will be determined by a number of factors, including the area's climate, the amount of direct sunlight the tank will receive, the type of soil it will be buried in if your storage system is underground, your budget, and how you want to use your water. If you don't have a tank yet, here are a few things you might want to consider before buying one:

- **Fiberglass tanks** are popular because they're reasonably-priced, durable, and lightweight. In addition, they can also be repaired quite easily when they crack. They come in standard sizes ranging from the very big to the very small, and can be bought as either horizontal or vertical cylinders. The biggest determining factor with fiberglass tanks will be the size you need, as smaller barrels are very expensive. Depending on regulations, a fiberglass tank might have to have an approved resin lining; if it's opaque in color, it can limit the growth of algae in the tank. Fiberglass tanks also come with the right fittings, which makes life easier for you, and ensures that you won't have leaks from ill-fitting fittings.

- **Polyethylene barrels** are commonly used in RWH systems and they come in any number of shapes, sizes, and colors. They can be used above or below ground—although the latter will have to be made of specially reinforced in-ground polyethylene to protect it from the pressure of expanding soil. They are relatively cheap and durable, and they are also lighter than most other tanks. When buying a polyethylene tank, it's best to go for a pigmented rather than a painted one. You should also consider the color of the tank and the impact this will have on the quality of your water; for instance, black tanks will inhibit algae growth, but they will also absorb more heat and may therefore have to be buried or placed in the shade. While the fittings for these tanks are easy to find, they may leak in some places if they aren't installed properly.

- **Metal tanks** — and especially galvanized metal — are popular because they are lightweight and easy to clean. They are available in small and medium sizes that can hold up to 2,500 gallons of water. If you want to use your water for drinking, cooking, and irrigating crops, the tank has to be lined with polyethylene, PVC, or an approved epoxy paint. This liner can also extend the longevity of your tank. The downside of metal tanks is that they can only be used above ground. In addition, if they are used with brass or bronze fittings, these can cause corrosion. Keep in mind that secondhand metal tanks may contain lead, so make sure you buy your tank from a trustworthy source.

- **Wood tanks** are popular, mostly for their aesthetic appeal. They are typically made of pine, cypress, or cedar that's held together by steel tension cables. In addition, they are also lined with plastic to make them more durable. Wood is a good insulating material, and this type of tank will keep your water cooler when it's hot and prevent it from freezing in winter. They are built on-site, and they can be taken apart and moved elsewhere. However, they can't be used underground or in hot, dry climates. Furthermore, wood tanks can also be expensive depending on the type of wood that's being used, and they're heavy and therefore more difficult and costly to transport.

- **Concrete tanks** are very versatile, as they can be made in any shape and size, and they can be used above or below ground. While prefabricated concrete tanks are available, they can also be cast in place—which means you can design yours however you want to. Also, the calcium in the concrete leaches into rainwater to reduce its corrosiveness and improve its taste. On the other hand, concrete tanks are susceptible to cracking—especially if they are underground. Additionally, tanks that have been built in place are considered permanent and they can't be moved or altered in any way. They also have to be lined with an appropriate and approved material if you want to have potable water.

There are many other materials available when it comes to rainwater storage tanks, including stone and ferro-cement—and if you want, you can even choose to use something else altogether such as a modified barrel, plastered tires, or a used swimming pool—in which to collect your rainwater. Other considerations when it comes to choosing a storage tank—such as potential maintenance, safety, and weather issues—is talked about in Chapter 8. The positioning of your tank is a very important decision, as it will determine not only the efficiency with which you can collect rainwater, but will also influence other factors, such as maintenance, cleaning, and safety. When you start designing your RWH system, keep in mind that water is heavy, so whatever you choose to store it in will have to be able to carry the weight.

Filters

"Filters" is quite a loaded term, and it can refer to anything from simple leaf screens to complex UV lights, water purifiers, or self-cleaning systems. In its simplest form, a filter is a component that removes particles—ranging from microscopic bacteria to large leaves and debris—from your water as it travels through the conveyance system. Depending on your needs and the resources you have available, it's up to you to make sure you choose the right filters, and also that you install them in places in your system where they'll have the most impact. For instance, if you want to create a potable water system or you struggle to keep your tank free of algae, you may have to consider installing UV lights to kill pathogens and purify your water. Similarly, if you have a big problem with sediment and sludge, you might have to consider using self-cleaning technology.

Rainwater can be filtered at various points along its journey through your RWH system, and the first place is between the catchment area and the tank. Cleaning rainwater before it enters the rain barrel typically involves removing debris— such as leaves and plant material— from the water. In addition to improving the overall quality of your water, filtering your water after it's left the roof will also help to reduce sludge buildup. Water can either be filtered by means of "diversion" or "screening."

Diversion: A First Flush Diverter

Roofs collect debris over time—especially when it's not raining—and if you're not careful, all of these contaminants and pollutants can end up in your water. This is where a first flush diverter—or "roof washer"—comes in handy, as it's a valve that diverts the first rain of the season away from your tank. This process is known as "diversion," because it prevents the first rainfall of the season—and all the debris that goes with it—from entering the tank. If you decide to install a first flush diverter, remember to clear the diverter chamber every time it has rained to make sure there's enough space for new debris to collect in it.

The best alternative to a first flush diverter is to install high-quality filters and UV lights that can prevent your water in your system from becoming polluted. On the other hand, you can also clean your roof regularly; however, this is not only a nuisance, but the heights and ladders involved can also threaten your safety.

If you choose to install a first flush diverter, you have many options to choose from—including DIY ideas! They can be basic or complex, depending on what you need, and the size of the diverter—and in particular its chamber—will depend on how much debris enters your system as a result of surrounding trees, rainfall intensity, dust collection, and other factors.

Screening: Leaf Screens

Screening prevents debris from entering the storage tank by filtering it out using screens. There are many types of screens that can be placed at various points along your conveyance system, including in the gutters, the downspout, and over the opening of your tank. Leaf screens are a particularly common type of screen found in RWH systems, and they can be installed wherever you find debris building up in your system. They are generally made of coarse mesh and they prevent leaves and other debris from entering your storage tank and contaminating your water. Depending on the intended use of your water, leaf screens are also vital in preventing the growth of algae and the accumulation of sludge. In addition, they prevent smaller animals and children from entering or falling into your water tank, and if the mesh is fine enough, they can even be used to keep mosquitoes out of your water. This is discussed in more detail in Chapter 7. It's important to regularly inspect and maintain your screens to see if they're still fastened securely. Also remember to clear them after rainfall events so that they don't become clogged up.

Water can also be treated after it's been stored and before it's put to use in and around the house; this is particularly important if you have a potable RWH system. In this phase, the focus is not just on removing debris, but also to disinfect water and to clear it of any microscopic contaminants and pollutants. More information about water quality and treatment is provided in Chapter 9.

ADDITIONAL COMPONENTS

The above parts are essential to every RWH system, but it doesn't have to end there. Your choices all depend on you and what you want, but before you can make these decisions, you first have to know what is available to you!

Pumps and Pump Controllers

In an ideal world, we'd need nothing more than gravity to get to our rainwater. Unfortunately, however, it may sometimes be necessary to install a pump in your RWH system. The purpose of a pump is to assist water flow from the storage tank to the place where you want to use it—such as your house and garden—and they're quite common in larger RWH systems. Deciding if you need a pump in your system will depend mostly on where your storage tank is located and what you want to use the water for. For example, an aboveground tank that is elevated in some way and is used to water the garden most likely won't need a pump, since the pressure created by gravity is enough to allow water to flow from through the hose. On the other hand, if you want to use the water in your house for domestic purposes such as cleaning, washing, bathing, and cooking, gravity alone may not give you the water pressure you need. In this case, you'll have to include a pump in your system. In addition, underground storage tanks will also require water pumps.

In a RWH system, a pump system doesn't merely refer to just the pump—oh no, it also includes the pressure tank, pressure switch, and check valve. The pump pulls water from the rainwater tank and stores it in pressurized form in the pressure tank until you're ready to use it. The water is prevented from flowing back into the storage tank by the one-way check valve. When a tap is opened and water flows out of it, the water pressure in the pressure tank drops; this activates the pump, which then begins pumping water again in order to maintain your water pressure. Some pumps push water, while others pull it; this will determine where you should place your pump relative to your storage tank. You can improve the efficiency of your pump system by regularly cleaning the filters and maintaining the pump. In addition, you can also reduce the strain on your pump and lower your electricity usage by placing larger pressure tanks in your system.

There are many different types of pumps available—and again, the type you choose will depend on your specific setup. Jet pumps use an electric motor and rotating impellers to create a vacuum suction that sucks the water from the storage tank, through the pump, and into the area where it's to be used. The suction force created by the pump is used to maintain the motion of sucking water, and therefore a jet pump has to be filled with water before it can be used. On the upside, these pumps are easy to transport, and they're also quite durable. They have to be placed on a level surface close to the water tank, and this makes them easy to access for maintenance purposes. They are also one of the cheaper options when it comes to water pumps.

Submersible pumps are submerged inside the water in the tank, from where they use centrifugal force to push water out of the tank. Because they are underwater, these pumps are much less noisy than jet pumps; in addition, they're also out of the way and won't become a potential eyesore. They're designed to be durable because they're likely to be placed in locations where access isn't easy; that being said, it can be difficult to inspect and maintain them when the time to do so comes. In addition, they are also more expensive than jet pumps.

Once you've decided what type of pump you want, you have to consider the size of the pump you'll need. A pump's size is calculated using "flow rate," which is the estimated amount of water you need for all the fixtures—such as showers, taps, hosepipes—you want to connect to your RWH system. Thus, the more fixtures you have in your system, the higher your flow rate, and the bigger the pump you'll need. Flow rate is measured in volume per time—most typically gallons per hour or gallons per minute.

In addition to your flow rate, the size of a pump is also influenced by the water pressure. Most water fixtures in a home function according to a predetermined water pressure, and if the water flows at a pressure that is lower than that, the fixtures won't work effectively. On the other hand, if water pressures exceed the maximum desired pressure of a fixture, the appliance might become damaged. Thus, it's important to know what range of pressures your fixtures require, so that you can choose the best pump for your system.

It's important to understand the flow rate and water pressure of a water pump, as these will be used to determine if you have the right pump or not. At the same time, you always have to understand the relationship between flow rate and water pressure: As the flow rate increases, the water pressure decreases. Thus, if you choose a pump with a higher value—such as water pressure—on one end, you have to understand that the corresponding value—flow rate—will decrease. Choosing the right pump is about balancing these two aspects until you find something that works for you. Thankfully, many RWH pump manufacturers supply their customers with charts and professional advice that can help you make the best decisions for your own system.

As seen above, the type of pump you'll choose is greatly influenced by the fixtures you want to attach it to. At the same time, it will also be impacted by the size of your RWH system, in particular the distances water has to be pumped through the conveyance system. "Dynamic head" refers to the water pressure in a RWH system relative to the width, length, and height of all the pipes in the system. Dynamic head is influenced by a number of factors, but one of the most important is "vertical lift," or the vertical distance that water has to be pumped from the rainwater storage tank. For instance, the vertical lift of a toilet on the second storey will be much higher than that of a tap on the ground floor, which will in turn require a larger pump to maintain adequate water pressure. Another factor that impacts dynamic head is "friction loss," which is the amount of energy required to pump water across horizontal distances. Simply speaking, the further water has to travel, the more friction loss it will have, and the more powerful the pump has to be. Additionally, friction loss is also influenced by the size of the pipes, and the amount of bends there are in the system.

Choosing the right pump can be complicated, but it's necessary to go through the process if you want to make the most of your RWH system. If your water pressure or flow is too low, for instance, you may find you're unable to use your harvested rainwater in the ways you wanted to. Alternatively, if your pump is not the right size, it can put unnecessary strain on its motor and burn out sooner than you had planned.

Monitoring Units

Although not a necessity, it can make your life easier to install monitoring units in your system in order to stay on top of the water levels, water pressure, and contaminants. For example, if you are dependent on your rainwater, you have to know how much you have left—and for this, you can use pressure transmitters to measure the hydrostatic pressure in your tank.

Secondary Storage

There will come a day when your RWH tank will be full— and then you'll wish you had planned for extra storage! Planning for overflow is important, not only because it will save you the sadness of seeing water go to waste, but also because it can help you prevent flooding and erosion. An important component in any overflow system is the overflow trap or outlet, which prevents water from flowing back into your storage tank. This is particularly important for underground tanks that can become damaged easily from too much overflow. Once additional water has been channeled out of the tank, it can be diverted into your garden to be used as irrigation, into your earthworks system, or into secondary storage tanks. Ideally, you shouldn't direct your overflow into the storm water system, as this means you lose precious rainwater and add additional pressure on the local infrastructure.

DESIGN CONSIDERATIONS

Every RWH system will be different depending on the needs of the people using it. Therefore, before you start designing yours, there are a few questions you have to ask yourself first:

- What do you want to use the water for?
- Will you want to expand your system later?
- How much rain can you collect in your area?
- If the tank overflows, where will the water go?
- Where will you position your tanks, and will they be placed above ground or underground?
- Can the tanks serve more than one purpose, such as providing shading for a garden, functioning as a windbreak, or serving as a structural component?
- Must the tanks be hidden for aesthetic reasons or to comply with local regulations?

- How will the water be diverted from the roof to the tank, and from the tank to the area where the water will be used?
- Is the system gravity-fed, or does it require a pump?

Now that you know everything a RWH system entails and you've started asking important design questions, it's time to dig a little deeper into your specific needs for RWH!

CHAPTER 5.A: SITE ANALYSIS
AND WATER QUALITY

There are many different aspects to designing a RWH system, which is why we've thought it best to divide all the different aspects into subchapters. In this subchapter, we look at how you can analyze the quality and the specific needs of your building site, your materials, and your rainwater volume, so that you can adapt your design and your building plans to what you have to work with.

SITE ANALYSIS

No two properties are the same, and if you want to design the most efficient RWH system possible, you have to make sure you do a complete site analysis. In her RWH guide, Patricia H. Waterfall (2004) suggests you begin by drawing a scale diagram of your property and all the elements on it, including the site boundaries, existing buildings, planted areas, paved areas, open spaces, and bodies of water. Once you've done this, you can note down existing drainage patterns as they occur when the rain falls. Walk on your property to get a better idea of the slopes, and look at erosion patterns to figure out how rainwater behaves on your site. These observations must not only include the high and low areas where the water flows and pools, but also which direction it moves in.

Slopes can be indicated as degrees from a horizontal line, as a ratio of its horizontal to its vertical distances, or as a percentage. In order to measure a gradient, you can use a bunyip water level or an A-frame, both of which are cheap and easy to build yourself. Generally, slopes and gradients are indicated as contour lines, which can be found on topographic maps.

Next, you can use this drawing to identify potential catchment areas, such as roofs, paving, and open spaces. Once you've done this, you can look for areas that may require irrigation, such as existing or new flower beds or vegetable gardens. Remember that RWH can also be done using earthworks, as discussed in Chapter 3—keep that in mind during this step of the process, and look out for places where you can include some of the tactics talked about earlier.

Now that you've identified where your water is coming from and where you want it to go, you can begin making plans to make it happen! Keep the following pointers in mind:

- Wherever possible, use gravity to move water from one point to another—this will reduce costs and electricity usage, as well as the time, energy, and money needed for pump maintenance and repairs.
- Try to locate storage tanks near planted areas.
- If your site is too big, or if you feel your system is becoming too complex, you can always divide it up into subsystems that can each be designed individually to tie in with the whole.
- Make sure you calculate your storage and conveyance requirements as accurately as possible— this is discussed next.

CHAPTER 5.B: CALCULATING FOR NEEDS AND SIZING

As with any kind of building and engineering, there's a lot of math involved in designing and constructing a working RWH system. If you're not someone whose regular job or career requires them to work with these kinds of calculations—such as a construction worker, architect, or engineer—you might find yourself confused about which calculations are necessary, what they mean, and what you need to do with the results! In this subchapter, we'll be laying out clear instructions for the calculations you need to do to make sure each and every component of your RWH system works properly.

RAIN VOLUME AND EXPECTED SUPPLY

If you want to know how much capacity your RWH system should have, it's important that you first work out how much rainfall you can expect to receive. This calculation should be done for each one of your catchment areas:

1. First, determine the area of your catchment area in square feet. For a roof, this means calculating the area of the building's footprint, and adding the area of the overhang.

Catchment area (in square foot) = Area of the building footprint + Area of the roof overhang

2. Once you've done this, calculate the estimated supply you can expect to receive by multiplying your catchment area (from above) with the amount of rainfall you can expect, the runoff coefficient, and 0.623. The number 0.623 is a constant, and it's a conversion factor used to convert inches of rainfall depth that falls over an area—in square foot—to volume in gallons. The rainfall depth will depend on the area you're in, and it can be found in RWH guides, or on the internet. The runoff coefficient is a predetermined number that is used to account for the type of surface your catchment area is made of. For example, roofing materials have much higher runoff coefficients than lawns because they don't absorb as much water. Runoff coefficients can be found in guidebooks, such as Patricia H. Waterfall's (2004) *Harvesting Rainwater for Landscape Use.*

Estimated harvested rainwater volume (in gallons) =
Catchment area (in square foot) x Rainfall depth (in inches) x
Runoff coefficient x 0.623

3. The figure you've calculated tells you how much rainwater you can expect to harvest in gallons. Remember to do this for each month so that you can get a better idea of how much rainfall your system will receive throughout the year and in different seasons.

EXPECTED DEMAND

While it's important for you to know how much water you can expect to harvest, you also have to know how much of it you will need. There are two ways to calculate the water demand for your garden—and don't worry, both are quite easy!

Method 1

This method can be used for both new and existing landscapes, and it should be done for each month. This calculation is based on the principle of evapotranspiration (ETo) which is a combined estimation of the amount of water a plant loses through its leaves, as well as how much moisture is lost through evaporation from soil surfaces. Simply put, ETo tells you how much water you'll need to irrigate your crops, and these figures can be found in guidebooks or on the internet. This equation combines ETo with a plant water use factor, which varies according to the type of plant in your garden. Again, this information is available in RWH guidebooks.

1. First, determine the ETo for your area, and multiply it with the plant factor.
2. Next, determine the size—in square feet—of the irrigated area, and multiply that with the number from above.
3. Multiply this with the 0.623 conversion factor.

Estimated water demand (in gallons) = (ETo x Plant factor) x Irrigated area (in square foot) x 0.623

Method 2

The following method can only be used for existing land-scapes, and it's based on how much water you've used in the past. For this calculation, you'll need to use your monthly water bills:

1. Separate your domestic water use from your outdoor water use: If you assume there's little to no irrigation in the winter months, then you can use this winter volume as the amount of water used indoors.

2. Assuming your indoor water use remains relatively stable throughout the year, any additional water use

in other months can then be considered as part of your irrigation.

3. Subtract your indoor use from the total use for every month; it's best to add these figures to a table such as the one below.

Month of the Year	Monthly Water Use (from water bill)	Indoor Water Use (will remain constant)	Outdoor Water Use (subtract indoor use from monthly use)

4. If your water bill is in cubic feet, remember to convert water volumes to gallons.

5. If you want to use your RWH system both for outdoor and domestic purposes, you can use your municipal water bill to estimate how much water you use in your house every month.

MUNICIPAL WATER NEEDS

Ideally, you'd want to irrigate your entire garden all year using rainwater. Unfortunately, there's a chance you'll have to continue relying on your municipal supply, even if it's only during the drier seasons. Using your supply and demand figures, you can estimate when and how much municipal water you'll need. To do this, create a "checkbook" with all the figures—supply and demand—for each month displayed next to each other, such as the one in Waterfall's (2004) RWH guide. Remember to include a column for "cumulative storage," which estimates how much water will be left over in your storage tank after you've met your water demands. When calculating your supply for the next month, add the leftover rainwater from the previous month. This will also give you an idea how much storage space you'll need in order to capture as much rainwater as possible. In months when you have no leftover storage and your demand is higher than your supply, you can determine how much municipal water you'll need. Below is an adaptation of Waterfall's checkbook:

Month of the Year	Supply (in gallons)	Demand (in gallons)	Water in Storage (supply minus demand)	Municipal Use(demand minus water in storage)

Think of this checkbook as a "water budget:" Whenever you're using water, you're spending it, and whatever you harvest is part of your income. If you save water in one month, it's carried over to the next, and if you spend more than you've made, you'll have a deficit that might require a loan from the municipality... it might be difficult to estimate these values at first, especially if you're new to RWH. However, don't be disheartened—the longer you do it, the more knowledgeable you'll become! That's why it's important to keep a logbook of all your water usage so that you can build up your information over time.

SIZING YOUR RWH SYSTEM

When deciding on a tank size, it's important to look at the relationship between your supply and demand. While knowing how much water you can harvest is necessary, it's also good to compare this information to how much of that water you plan to use, and when. For instance, if you plan to use all of your water as soon as it's harvested, you most likely won't run into overflow problems, unless you receive very heavy rain. On the other hand, if you want to save some of your water for times when it's drier, you might have to consider larger storage capacity. This is especially important if you plan to use your water both indoors and outdoors.

The previous section shows you how to calculate your supply; however, keep in mind that this is an ideal figure, and it's likely your system won't be 100% efficient. For instance, some water may be lost to first flush diverters, leakages, evaporation, or spillage, or the surface of your catchment area may be more absorbent than the calculator factors in. For this reason, it's safe to assume an efficiency rate of 75 % to 90% when calculating your estimated water supply. When choosing a tank size, here are a two rules provided to us by industry experts:

- If your demand is less than your supply, the size of your tank will be determined by the amount of water you have leftover.
- If your supply is more than your demand, your tank size will be decided by the largest cumulative amount of water you can store in the year. If this is the case, you'll also have to keep in mind that you might have to supplement your water supply in other ways.

It's important that the size of your barrel fits your needs, but bigger doesn't always equal better. While some homesteaders have a lot of space available, many people—especially those who live in urban environments—don't have that luxury. Furthermore, if you live in a rental, you might want a barrel that's small enough to take with you should you decide to move. If you want a small barrel but have enough space available, you can even consider installing more than one barrel to increase your storage capacity. In this regard, it's estimated that more than three barrels aren't cost-effective.

Finally, keep in mind that whatever barrel you choose has to be able to fit through gateways and doorways—there's no point in buying a tank if you can't get it onto your property! A small barrel might not be ideal for your needs, and there's a possibility you won't be able to harvest all the rainwater you receive. That being said, it's still better to collect some rainwater than none at all.

Keep in mind that annual rainfall figures aren't always accurate, especially with current global season changes. It's impossible to be prepared for everything, but knowing that you could receive more or less water than you expected can help you plan what you should do if your system overflows, or if you run out of water. For example, if you're concerned about not having enough water, you can use water conservation strategies in your home, optimize your garden with hard landscaping, start using gray water outdoors, or increase your catchment area by adding rain barns or outbuildings to your property. Remember, if your irrigation needs are much higher than your expected supply, you can also use earthworks to capture more rainwater in your garden.

CHAPTER 5.C: GUIDELINES AND BEST PRACTICES

Now is the moment you've been waiting for! After going through the components of a functional RWH system, your required calculations, and the environmental factors you need to consider, we're going to talk about best practices for actually designing a working RWH system that suits your needs—whether it's irrigating your garden, storing rainwater as a backup to your main water source, or anything else you have in mind.

LOCATING YOUR RAIN BARREL

For the most part, the locations of the various components in your RWH system have been decided for you: Unless you're starting from scratch, your catchment area—especially if it's a roof—gutters, downspouts, and garden have already been laid out. If your RWH system is new, however, you'll have to find the perfect place for your rain barrel—and while it may sound daunting, it's the perfect opportunity to find a way to connect the different elements of your system in an efficient and logical way.

When it comes to connecting your rain barrel to the rest of your RWH system, there are two important factors you have to consider. The first is its proximity to your downspouts, and the second is its location relative to the water's final destination, such as a garden or pump. Ideally, you'd want to locate your barrel as close as possible to the downspout so that it can be filled up easily. That being said, if this place is very far away from your garden for instance, it may easier to move the water from the tank to its final destination than it is to transfer it from your conveyance system to the tank— the last thing you want is to have a complicated system of pipes running all across your property to the end-use area. If your storage tank is far from your downspouts, you can use pipes to connect these different elements with each other, provided all the pipes you use slope at a downward angle.

If you don't have gutters and downspouts, fear not! It's possible to collect rainwater straight from your roof—all you have to do is place your barrel underneath the roof at the place where you see the most water flowing down it. In order to do this effectively, you'll have to spend some time observing the rainfall patterns on your roof before you decide where to locate your tank. Typically, the most water will collect in corners of the low points of valleys on roofs.

A further aspect to consider is how easy it is to access your rain barrel. Remember, you'll have to maintain it quite regularly, so if it's a nightmare to get to, or if there's very little space around it, this may cause some problems in the future. If you simply want to use your tank as a tap or something to connect a hosepipe to, you should also keep in mind that it has to be accessible. When you design your RWH system, try to imagine how the water will be transferred from the tank to the place where you want to use the water: Would you have to walk very far to fill up a bucket or watering can? Is there enough space under the spigot to place your bucket or watering can? Will your pump have to work very hard to move water through a complicated system of pipes? Will your hose pipe be able to reach your garden, and will there be any obstacles in its way? There are also a few other requirements for the location of a rain barrel:

- It has to be on level ground.
- If you plan to put it on a platform, make sure that platform is sturdy enough to carry not only the weight of the barrel, but also the weight of the water once it has been filled up.
- Your tank should be in a place you can get it to: There's no use choosing a location only to find later that your gateways or openings are too small for it to fit through!

- There can't be any water around your tank—
  especially pools of still-standing water—as this will
  attract mosquitoes.
- If your rainwater tank is unsightly, and this is
  something that bothers you, you can locate it in a
  place where it will be hidden. It can also be covered
  with a screen or a hedge, for instance, but keep in
  mind that you should still have access to it after
  you've covered it.

Along with rainwater, gravity is one of nature's greatest gifts
—so use it! Because of water's weight, it exerts pressure on
itself which makes it flow faster; this is called "head pressure." The more water you have in your tank, the heavier it'll
be, and therefore, the faster it'll flow and the higher your
water pressure will be. Head pressure is important—especially if you don't have a pump—because without it, you
might not be able to connect a hosepipe to it. One way to
increase head pressure is to elevate your tank. Another way
is to have a higher, narrower tank, as opposed to a wider,
shallower one. Elevating your tank will also give you easier
access to the spigot because it increases the amount of space
you have available to place a bucket under it, or to connect a
hosepipe. Even if you don't elevate your tank, it's important
that it still be uphill from the final destination of the water, if
possible. Of course, if your tank is underground, this isn't an
option, and using the advantages of head pressure and
gravity won't be an option.

It's important to keep your rain barrel free of debris as much as possible. Hence, when it comes to choosing the location of your barrel, it's best to choose a place where this won't be a problem. For instance, placing your barrel directly underneath trees or a roof that is likely to collect a lot of debris and pollutants can become problematic. One way to get around this problem is to cover the top of your tank with a mesh screen to filter out debris before it enters the water in your tank. If covering your tank isn't enough, you can also add screens to your gutters and downspouts, or install a first flush diverter to help you steer clear of all the contaminants that collect on a roof during dry seasons.

We don't always have a large number of options available to us when it comes to choosing a location for your tank, but try to put it in the shade, if at all possible. The reason for this is that algae needs the sun to grow, so removing sunlight from your tank can go a long way to resolving algae-related problems. Having an opaque tank will also help you with this problem. Another reason is that some barrels can leach chemicals into your rainwater if they're placed in the sun. As for the longevity and durability of your barrel, the sun emits harmful UV rays that can damage most materials, especially if they haven't been treated for this purpose. Unless your tank has a special UV coating on it, it's best to keep it in the shade.

FIRST FLUSH DIVERTERS

It's been said before, but it deserves repeating: First flush diverters work! They help to keep your water clean and free of contaminants, and they also prevent blockages from occurring in your conveyance system. They'll reduce the amount of sludge buildup in your tank, which will in turn reduce the time, energy, and money required to remove this sludge and maintain your rainwater tank. They also prevent fittings such as spigots and filters from becoming blocked or damaged. Most importantly, they can protect your pump from sediment and increase its longevity.

A first flush diverter doesn't have to be expensive or complicated—it's possible to build one using simple and inexpensive materials from your local hardware store. While many agree that first flush diverters are a must-have, there are a few things you should consider before designing, building, or installing one:

- The sizing of your diverter is important, because it has to be able to accommodate the duration and intensity of a typical rainfall event. If your first flush is too big, you can waste precious rainwater and even struggle to fill up your tanks. On the other hand, if your diverter is too small, it will be unable to divert the necessary water, and the debris that was meant to be diverted will end up in your water tank anyway. Other factors to take into account when trying to decide what the optimal size for your first flush diverter should be include the size, slope, and material of your roof, the size of your gutters, and the time between rainfall events.

- First flush diverters require a lot of maintenance, so be prepared for this! If you want your diverter to function effectively, you have to clean it out regularly; scheduling the maintenance of this component is discussed in Chapter 8.

- There are people who consider first flush diverters to be a weak point in a RWH system because their exposed nature makes them susceptible to the whims of different temperatures. If it's too cold, your diverter might freeze and crack; at the same time, too much exposure to the sun will degrade whatever material your first flush diverter is made of. Sadly, there are few ways to get around this: The best is to inspect it regularly to make sure it hasn't become damaged, and to prepare yourself for the additional work that comes with this part of a RWH system.

- While the debris that a first flush diverter removes isn't ideal for a potable water system, your garden might actually love the organic material that collects on your roof. This is good news, because it means if you design your system smartly, you can use the water from a first flush for irrigation so that it won't go to waste.

- If all of this sounds overwhelming, you can always prevent debris from entering your water by removing your downspout at the beginning of the first rainfall event of the season, and replacing it once your roof has been cleaned.

GENERAL GUIDELINES AND IDEAS

There are hundreds of different ways to harvest rainwater, and the choices you eventually make should depend on what you want and need from your RWH system. In order to help you with your decisions, here are a few general things you can consider when designing, installing, using, and maintaining your RWH system:

- If you can't harvest enough rainwater in your area, it's possible to install a dual supply system that supplements harvested rainwater with water from your local municipality. This can be especially helpful during seasons when there is little or no rainfall, or if you'd prefer to install only a non-potable system and continue getting your potable water from the public water service.
- Some states have created incentives for homesteaders who harvest rainwater—if you find yourself in one of those states, do the research so you can make sure you reap the benefits of your hard work!

- On the flip side, some states have serious regulations when it comes to RWH systems. If you're unsure what the policies are in your area, flip to Chapter 2 for more information about this.

- It's important that you take your site analysis and supply and demand calculations seriously, because if you get it wrong, you might have to redo parts of your RWH system—or worse, redesign it from scratch all over again.

- If you're working with existing components, remember that they can always be adapted to suit your needs better. For instance, roofs and shading structures can be enlarged to increase your catchment area, or existing gutters can be moved and changed to better fit the placement of your rainwater barrel.

- We all want to be in a position where we can irrigate our entire garden with rainwater, but for some of us, it simply won't be possible. If supplementing your water system with municipal water isn't an option and you find you need more water for your garden, you can always consider reducing the size of your planted area, incorporating more hard landscaping, or using waterwise plants that require less water.

- If you're designing your garden from scratch, keep in mind the amount of water you can harvest when deciding how big the garden should be and what types of plants you want to use.

- Although it's not discussed in extensive detail here, you can always supplement your water needs with gray water.
- When in doubt, turn to the experts: There's a reason why people specialize in certain RWH components—especially the more intricate ones, such as purifiers, filters, and pumps—so don't disregard the value some outside guidance can have. Homesteaders are crafty and clever people, but there's no shame in asking for help!

It's good to know what the best practices are in the world of RWH, but even so, problems often do arise. If this happens, don't become disheartened—the spirit of a true homesteader is to find creative and unique ways to resolve challenges! Now that you've informed yourself as much as possible,you're in a better position to make the right decisions. It's time to start thinking about the installation of your RWH system!

CHAPTER 6: DIY INSTALLATION

Sure, if you have the funds, you can easily hire someone to build a RWH system for you, but where's the fun in that? Homesteaders are an independent, crafty bunch, and if you count yourself among them, you're probably someone who values your ability to do it yourself. In this chapter, we talk about some of the things you need to remember if you want to grab your toolbox and put your RWH system together yourself in order to reduce the chances you'll have to rip it down and start over again. If you were taking notes on your site analysis, calculations, and design plans as you went through previous chapters, grab that notebook again now, because we'll be taking all those calculations and considerations into account as we work through this chapter!

THE SECRET BEHIND RAIN BARRELS

No RWH system can function without a place to store the water, which means your rain barrel is a pretty important part of your design. There are many ways to get your hands on a rain barrel—you can buy a new one, use a secondhand one, or you can repurpose something else and use it to build your own storage tank. If you have the right materials on hand, the last option in particular is quite attractive, because it's easy, cheap—and most of all, fun! But how to go about doing this?

First of all, you have to find a container. This is probably the most important step, because if your rain barrel is wrong, you'll have nothing but problems in the future. For a tank to be appropriate, it has to comply with a number of requirements:

- It has to be made of a material that won't leach contaminants into your water, such as a barrel made of food-grade plastic.
- Remember that water is very heavy, so it has to be strong enough to carry the weight and withstand the pressure.
- It can't have been used to store any harmful chemicals in the past.
- It's best if it's opaque—even if it's painted—to keep out pesky algae.

- It must be big enough to meet your needs and store all the water you want to harvest.
- Ideally, it must have a lid of some sort—even if it's a mesh screen—to keep out debris, mosquitoes, and other animals, and to minimize the risk of children falling into the water.
- It can't have any openings that will result in leakages.

Assembling a Rain Barrel

If you're a DIY type of homestead, there's no doubt you're excited to get your hands dirty—and luckily for you, the moment has finally arrived! In addition to a barrel, you'll also need a few other things. These include:

- an outdoor faucet.
- an adhesive you can use as a sealant, such as silicone.
- a downspout and/or downspout extender that fits the size of the downspout.
- an overflow outlet, such as rubber tubing, a hose pipe, or a PVC pipe.
- an extension for your overflow.
- a conduit nut that fits the overflow outlet.
- plumber's tape to use on threaded joints.
- a mesh screen, if the top of your barrel is open.
- tools you can use to drill and cut holes in the tank.
- something to mark the positions and sizes of the holes, such as a marker.

Once you've gotten your materials, grab your tools and materials so you can start building! Assembling a rain barrel is very easy with these steps:

1. Make sure the barrel is clean, and that there is no leftover residue inside it. You can sand your barrel lightly and paint it with latex paint or spray paint to make the plastic more durable. You can also improve its aesthetics by covering it with another material, such as wood.

2. Move your barrel to the location you have chosen when designing your RWH system. If you've decided to elevate your barrel, construct the platform using your chosen materials.

3. Measure the distance between the gutter and the downspout, and mark and cut a hole in the top of the barrel that is large enough to insert the downspout. Seal the edges of the hole using sealant. Follow the instructions of the sealant very carefully, and make sure it's dried completely.

4. If the top of your barrel is open, cut the mesh to the same size of your barrel and place it over the opening.

5. To build the water outlet, you'll need to make a hole for the faucet, line the hole with sealant, and insert the faucet into the hole. If your faucet has threaded joints, remember to wrap them with plumber's tape before you screw the different components together.

RAINWATER HARVESTING FOR YOUR HOMESTEAD | 121

It's also important that the faucet is screwed in as tightly as possible.

6. To construct an overflow, drill a hole the size of the overflow near the top of the barrel. Screw the overflow pipe into the hole and seal its edges using sealant. To make sure the overflow is in place tightly, you can screw a conduit nut to the pipe on the inside of the barrel.

7. Extend the overflow to the place you want any extra water to go, such as another barrel, a flowerbed or vegetable garden.

If you've decided to use multiple barrels, you can also connect them yourself. To do this, follow the same steps you did when connecting the overflow to the tank. As for the installation of the rainwater pump, this will depend on the type and specifications of the pump you've bought.

CHAPTER 7: THE SEVEN BIGGEST MISTAKES OF RWH

E veryone makes mistakes, but some errors are avoidable—and when you're putting time, money, and energy into a RWH system, learning from the experience of others is more convenient than learning from trial and error. It's also cheaper to prevent breakdowns from occurring instead of fixing them after the fact! For that reason, in this chapter, we'll look at seven common mistakes people make when building their RWH system and how you can get things done right the first time.

On his YouTube channel, survival gardening expert David The Good (2016) talks about the seven biggest mistakes people make when installing collection systems. Below, each of these are outlined, as well as what you can do to avoid them.

Remember: The purpose of a RWH system is to *save* you money, not to cost you money! While an initial investment is necessary, the initial cost of a RWH system should never outweigh the money you will save in the long-term.

UNNECESSARY EXPENSES ON YOUR RWH SYSTEM

The first mistake many people make when installing a RWH system is spending too much money on it. Collecting rainwater is not free, and it's definitely worthwhile to invest in this practice. At the same time, overcomplicating the system can result in unnecessary expenses that could easily have been avoided.

There are many components to a RWH system, and the system itself can be as complex or as simple as you want it to be. While more complex systems may be more efficient in some circumstances, bigger is not always better. Depending on what you want to do with your harvested rainwater, some systems do not have to consist of anything more than large barrels. To quote David The Good (2016), "It is better to harvest some, and do it on the cheap, than to harvest none." If your system is too expensive, it may discourage you from installing it—and this means you will miss out on all the benefits of RWH.

In order to calculate the "payback time" of your RWH system, Martinson and Thomas (2007) give the following four steps that people can follow. Firstly, they suggest you determine how much money you currently spend on water, and how much of that money can be saved if you install a RWH system. If this is your first time collecting your own rainwater, it may be difficult to determine how much water you can get from your system and how effectively you can put it to use. However, this amount can be estimated using the size of the cistern you plan to install, and the amount of rainwater your area receives. Because the amount of rain will vary according to the season, it is best to calculate this amount as an average of the amount of money you can save per year.

In the next step, you have to estimate how much it will cost you to build or install your RWH system. Once you have calculated this figure using the system you have designed for yourself in Chapter 5, you can divide the cost of the system by the money you will save on water, and voila—you have calculated your payback time!

Depending on how much your system will cost, it may take you months, or even years, to make your money back. Remember, however, that a RWH system is about more than just saving money: It also saves the environment, reduces stress on local infrastructure, and makes sure we have a future in which water does not become an unavailable resource.

If you feel that your payback time is too long—or if the cost of installing a RWH system is more than you can spend right now—there are a few simple steps you can take to reduce the cost of your RWH system, or to make sure you are not spending unnecessary money. Firstly, you have to make sure the size of your cistern is not too big. It is important to have a large enough tank to make sure you collect as much rainwater as you possibly can, and there's nothing worse than watching a tank overflow and precious water going to waste. However, if you overestimate how much rainwater you can harvest, you may end up with a large and expensive tank that does nothing for your system other than waste space and money.

A second step you can take to lower the cost of RWH is to reduce how much money you spend on the construction of your system. This can be done by using cheaper materials, as well as building and installing the system yourself instead of paying laborers to do it for you. RWH systems don't always have to be made of components specifically intended for that use—it is possible to design an entire system using cheaper materials you can easily find from your local hardware store. However, if you decide to do this, keep in mind that not all barrels can be used to collect rainwater. For instance, barrels that once contained poisonous or toxic chemicals are contaminated and may make your water unsuitable for your home or garden. That being said, RWH doesn't have to be unaffordable—with a little creativity and research, anyone can do it!

MOSQUITOES IN YOUR RWH SYSTEM

Mosquitoes love to breed in standing water, and unfortunately, rainwater tanks are no exception. But why is this a bad thing? One of the reasons why mosquitoes in your drinking water is dangerous is because they carry pesticides from the environment directly into your home—and your body. Very few people enjoy having these pesky little bugs around, and there are many poisons and toxins available that aim to get rid of them. Sadly, these substances can make their way into your RWH system and pollute your water as a result. Another reason why you don't want mosquitoes in your rainwater is because they can carry viruses and diseases and cause you and your family to become ill.

Mosquitoes are everywhere and difficult to control—so how do you prevent them from breeding in your RWH system? It is important to do regular checks on your water tank to make sure your water has not become a breeding site for mosquitoes. To be safe, it is best to do this every three months; if you see any larvae floating in your tank, it is time to think of strategies to get rid of them.

The easiest way to keep mosquitoes out of your tank is to cover it with netting or a removable insect screen. In some places, the specifics of these screens may be regulated such as the size of the mesh or the material that the screen is made of. Even if there are no regulations, however, it is best to make sure you get an effective screen that can keep your water and your household safe. Furthermore, when you install a screen, make sure that *all* openings into the tank are sealed, including gutters, downpipes, overflow and inflow pipes, vents, and any gaps around the lid of the tank around pipe entry points. Additionally, these screens and sealants should be inspected and maintained regularly to ensure they remain efficient. The good news is that a screen will not only help keep out mosquitoes, but it will also keep your tank free of other debris that can clog up your pipes and make its way into your water.

When it comes to mosquitoes, it's also important to make sure that there are no bodies of standing water near your RWH system, including any drainage from the tank that causes puddles to form around the tank. Remember that mosquitoes can breed in as little as one to two inches of standing water, so even the smallest puddle can attract them!

If your specific RWH system allows for it, you can put fish in your tank to control mosquitoes in your rainwater. The most popularly used fish for this purpose are mosquito fish because they eat mosquito larvae. They can tolerate a reasonable range of water temperatures, and they require a minimum tank size of 10 gallons. Although they are relatively easy to take care of, it is important to make sure no chemicals or pesticides enter their water. Because of their hardiness, mosquito fish can easily outcompete other fish; this means many countries consider them an invasive species. Thus, it is important to never, ever release them into natural bodies of water unless they are native to that area. For those who do not want to use mosquito fish, goldfish are just as effective at controlling mosquitoes as they also feed on mosquito larvae.

Mosquitoes can also be controlled by chemical means. One way of doing this is to add vegetable oil to your RWH tank. This method is effective because the oil floats on top of the water and traps mosquitoes when they try to land in your rainwater. There are many types of oil you can use—including olive oil, horticultural oil, and dormant oil—and the amount of oil will depend on the size of your tank. However, oil can potentially clog up your system over time, so be careful if you do decide to use this method to control mosquitoes.

A final way to manage mosquitoes is to use "mosquito dunks." These are typically round in form and they contain a naturally occurring bacteria known as *bacillus thuringiensis israelensis* that controls mosquito breeding in standing water. Dunks are tasteless and odorless, and they pose no danger to other insects or to plants. They work by being placed inside the water where they will dissolve slowly. When using dunks, it is important to check on them regularly and replace them when needed. Furthermore, when choosing a dunk, it is best to go for one that sinks rather than floats, as floating dunks can be washed out of the tank if it becomes overfilled with water.

CHOKING YOUR BARREL'S FLOW

It is one thing to harvest rainwater, but another thing entirely to get it out of your tank. If it takes too long for you to retrieve water, chances are you won't get the best use out of your RWH system... and you might even decide to abandon the idea altogether. This is why it's very important to make sure you attach a spigot to your tank, and that you choose the right size spigot so that you can get quick and easy access to all of your collected rainwater.

There are a few things to consider when choosing a spigot for your rainwater barrel. Firstly, you have to think of the water pressure of your system: If you have a pressurized system, having a small opening valve won't pose as big a problem. However, if your system is not pressurized, having a small spigot will choke the flow of your system and bring you nothing but frustration. You also have to consider how you intend to use the water, as attaching a hosepipe to the tank will further decrease the flow rate of the water. Something else to keep in mind is that debris—such as leaves and twigs—may enter your tank. The smaller your valve is, the easier it will be for it to become blocked, and cleaning it can be somewhat of a nightmare. At the same time, it is easier to clear debris from a larger valve, as the force of the water will most likely wash out anything that may be blocking it.

Barrels and valves can also become choked if there is too much debris in the tank. This can be avoided by regularly cleaning your gutters and downspouts. It is also important to remember to clean your roof—especially after dry periods. The best way to avoid clogging up your system with dirt and animal feces is to allow the first rainspell to clean your roof, and to wait 10 minutes before you start collecting water. If this isn't possible, you can also install a diverter in your system, which will direct the first rainwater away from your system.

While some barrels may come with a standard-sized spigot, these are not necessarily always ideal and may be far too small. This can easily be remedied by buying a different spigot, or by constructing your own—thankfully, there are many resources that can teach you how to make your own valve so that you can get the most out of your RWH system!

LETTING RAINWATER GO TO WASTE

There is no worse feeling than watching precious rainwater go to waste while your tank is overflowing... one of the biggest mistakes you can make when installing a RWH system is to design one that does not have enough capacity. At the same time, installing a system that is too big will result in you spending unnecessary money and making the process of RWH too expensive. In order to avoid making these mistakes, there are certain calculations you can do when designing your RWH system—see Chapter 5.B for more information on these.

If you are not using a barrel specifically designed for RWH, it is also important to make sure it doesn't leak before you install it. Losing water through a leaky barrel is disheartening, and it means you will miss out on one of nature's most precious resources.

In addition to using tanks that are too small, a further mistake people make when harvesting rainwater is installing an overflow that is too small, or not installing one at all. If your overflow is not the right size, water may spill out of your tank if a lot of water is entering it at once. Some tanks are already equipped with an overflow, but that is not to say it is the appropriate size for your system. Instead, make sure your overflow is the same size as the pipe that feeds the water into the tank.

RAINWATER HARVESTING FOR YOUR HOMESTEAD | 133

Even if your overflow is the right size, its purpose will be meaningless if there's nowhere for the water to go. Think of where the water will be directed once it leaves the overflow pipe: Is it going to a place where it can be of use—such as a garden bed or a swale—or is it being sent down a driveway, road, or even a lawn where it will simply disappear into the main stormwater drainage system? Even worse, are you dumping water next to your tank where it can soak into the foundation and create puddles that are the perfect breeding ground for mosquitoes? Designing a RWH system means taking into account *all* possible scenarios—including what will happen if your tank receives more water than you expected. It doesn't have to be difficult or costly; a little research into the appropriate landscaping and material use can help you make sure you don't miss out on any precious rainwater.

Finally, remember to *use* your rainwater once you have collected it. It's never a good idea to waste water, but if you are too conservative about how you use it, you may find that you can't collect any more water when the rain starts falling again. The key here is to put it to good use in and around your house. It is also helpful to have an estimate of how much water you can collect in a season and how much you typically use; this way you can plan your water use in such a way that you won't run out while still maximizing the rainfall opportunities that come your way.

USING SWALES TO HARVEST RAINWATER

Swales are trenches that you can dig along the contour lines of your garden, and they are discussed in more detail in Chapter 4. No matter how efficient your RWH system, there will always be surface runoff that won't find its way into your garden. Typically, rainwater will run downhill and make its way into a stream, river, or even the road, where it will evaporate or be taken away from your property. Using swales, however, can prevent this water from being lost. Instead, it will soak into your ground and irrigate your plants and crops. In addition, surface runoff also brings organic matter with it. This can be trapped by a swale and used to fertilize the soil in your garden.

Not everyone can build swales: If you don't have a slope in your garden, for instance, or if your property isn't big enough, this might not be accessible to you. However, for those who do have the gradient and space to build swales, do it—and don't miss out!

ALGAE IN YOUR RWH SYSTEM

Algae are very small single-celled aquatic plants that grow underwater in places where the conditions are suitable. These plants do not have roots, leaves, stems, or flowers, but like other plants, they contain chlorophyll and therefore need sunlight to photosynthesize. Algae can grow in a wide variety of water conditions, and they ideally require a minimum of 10 hours of sunlight a day. They also prefer warmer water that doesn't receive too much turbulence. If you plan to use your rainwater to water your garden or irrigate your crops, algae poses no threat. In fact, it can even serve as compost for your soil and make the ground more fertile. If you want to put your water through a filtration system, however, algae can clog up the various components and cause you nothing but trouble. It can also block overflow valves and hosepipes. Therefore, it is important to make sure you don't allow algae to grow in your RWH tank.

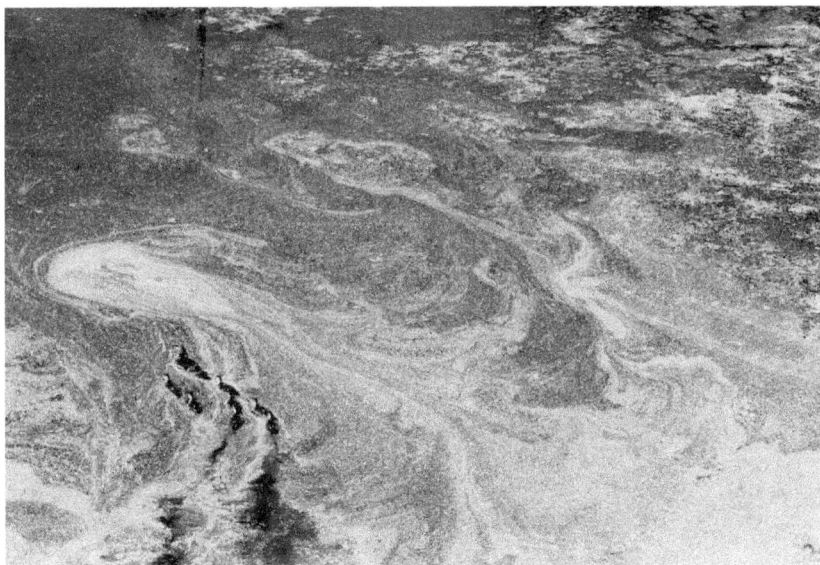

Despite the harm that algae can cause to your RWH system, it is very easy to get rid of this problem—simply cut off the sunlight they need to photosynthesize! For those who haven't installed a system yet, you can consider buying a tank that is made of a material that specifically blocks out light. However, if you already have a tank, fear not—there are a few simple things you can do to solve your algae problems:

- Placing your tank in the shade will block sunlight to make sure the algae doesn't receive the sunlight they need to grow.
- White barrels that allow sunlight in can be painted black to block out the light and starve the algae of sunlight.
- You can clean your tank at least once—but preferably three times—a year with dishwashing liquid and hot water to remove existing algae and prevent it from growing again. It is best to do this in the fall before the start of the rainy season.
- Because algae prefers stable conditions, using your water at least once every five to seven days can cause enough turbulence to prevent algae from growing.
- Dirty gutters and downspouts equal dirty, algae-filled barrels, so make sure you clean your gutters regularly—especially after a heavy rainstorm. Clean gutters will also ensure that rainwater can flow more freely and that the water that does enter your tank is clean.

- Rain barrel screens are used to catch any debris and prevent it from entering the tank, but if your screen is dirty, it can create an ideal environment for algae to grow in. To avoid this, make sure you clean your rain barrel screens often.
- If you go through periods when your rain barrels are empty—such as winter—you can store them upside down to prevent bacteria and algae from getting into them.
- UV filters can be set up in a RWH system to keep the water clean.
- Adding a quarter teaspoon of bleach per one gallon of water to your tank will kill microorganisms in the water, such as algae. You can also use a diluted bleach solution to clean the insides of your rain barrels,

then rinse them out before using them for water storage again.

- A small amount of chlorine—four parts to 1,000,000 parts rainwater—will get rid of algae while at the same time ensuring the water is still safe to use in your house and garden. It is important to follow these ratios very carefully, and to not use both bleach and chlorine in your water; while small amounts of these chemicals are not harmful, too much can make your water unusable.
- For a more natural solution, a 1:1 ratio of white vinegar to water can be used to clean out rain barrels.

Similar to rain barrels, algae can also grow in rainwater collection ponds. Follow these strategies to make sure your pond stays free of algae:

- Aquatic plants—such as lily pads, lotus, watercress, or cattails—use up the nutrients algae need to grow, and therefore starve them. Floating plants will also decrease the amount of sunlight that enters your pond. In addition, these plants will beautify your pond and turn it into a pleasant feature in your garden.
- If you have fish in your pond, make sure to not overfeed them, as the nutrients from the excess food creates the perfect environment for algae to grow.

You can also buy special types of fish food that is made specifically to discourage algae from growing in your pond.

- Certain water treatments can be used to control algae growth; if you do decide to use this method, keep in mind that the treatments have to be repeated regularly and that the dosage instructions have to be followed very closely.

Algae can be a problem, but it can also be solved quite easily, so there's no reason to give up on your RWH dreams!

MISSING OUT ON RAINWATER ALTOGETHER

The biggest mistake you can possibly make when it comes to RWH is to not collect any rainwater at all. Rain is a precious gift from the sky that we can't afford to pass up on—especially in times such as ours when there are more droughts and water is becoming increasingly scarce all over the world. Designing and installing a RWH system requires time, money, and energy, but it's all worth it in the end. Unlike chlorinated municipal water, rainwater is much healthier for your plants—and it's also free!

With these things in mind, it is time to start thinking about the maintenance of your RWH system. Like all things, this technology has to be maintained after it has been installed—and Chapter 8 will teach you how!

CHAPTER 8: SAFETY AND MAINTENANCE

L et's say you've built your ideal RWH system following all of the dos and don'ts from previous chapters. At last, you're using rainwater to irrigate your garden, fill your toilet tanks, and top up your fountains, and it's feeding beautifully into any other professionally-installed systems you may have. Thanks to your new RWH setup, your homestead is thriving more than ever before... but if you want your system to continue serving its purpose in the long term, you need to maintain it. Not only that, but as is always the case when it comes to water, health and safety is also a concern you have to take into consideration. In this chapter, we'll discuss both these aspects of RWH, as well as all the things you'll need to keep in mind when maintaining your system.

MAINTAINING THE DIFFERENT COMPONENTS

A RWH system consists of more than one component; therefore, there is more to maintain than just the tank. Over time, all of the various parts that make up the system will have to be kept up or replaced, but some elements are more important than others. If you don't maintain your RWH system regularly, it can cause frustration, and even put your health in danger. Low water pressure, poor water quality, contamination, clogged filters, blocked pipes, and pump failure are just some of the many problems that can arise if RWH system maintenance is not prioritized. Below is a list of all the components that will require maintenance and how often they should be checked, as well as what you need to do to make sure your RWH system functions as efficiently as it possibly can.

The Roof

It's not easy to clean a roof, and often it can't be done safely. However, if it is accessible to you, it is best to inspect your roof for the buildup of debris and waste materials and to clear these materials, if possible. This is particularly important if you don't have a first flush diverter or if it's impossible for you to divert the first rain after a dry season away from your tank. The best time to do this is before the season's first rainstorm—but it should only be done if you can do it safely!

If you find that there are any tree branches overhanging your roof and gutters, it is best to prune these so that the roof is clear of all obstacles and potential sources of debris. Installing a RWH system can add to the load carried by your roof, so it is important to occasionally inspect your roof's structural integrity.

Gutter, Pipes, and Fittings

Gutters have to be cleaned and inspected at least once every six months. However, if you find that they become clogged regularly, you'll have to clean them more often. When maintaining your gutters, you always have to make sure they're still securely fastened in place—water is heavy, and brackets or ties that have become loosened can lead to damage and injury on your property. If your gutters are subjected to the weather, they may become worn over time. This might cause leakages, which you'll have to fix if you want to keep your RWH system as efficient as possible.

Downpipes aren't as easy to clean as gutters because they're not as accessible. That being said, if you suspect one of them may have become blocked, you have to remove the blockage as soon as possible to prevent any further damage. The best time to do this is during a rainfall event, because you'll be able to see how effective your system is functioning, and if there are any places where the water is flowing slower than it normally would. Depending on the material your pipes and fittings are made of, they may also begin to leak over time. Thus, if you want to make sure you don't lose any precious water, inspect all pipe and fitting connections regularly and repair anything that's broken.

Filters

Your filters are installed to remove debris and pollutants from your tank—in other words, they were made to get dirty! Clogged filters will not only slow down the flow of water in your system, but it also reduces their efficiency and puts you and your family at higher risk for waterborne diseases. There are many types of filters, and each has their own specific maintenance requirements. As a general rule, however, it's best to clean your filters every three to six months, or directly after heavy rainfall events. Mesh filters can be cleaned fairly easily by removing them from the system and rinsing them with water. More complex filters, such as UV filters, will most likely have manufacturer's requirements that you should follow to ensure you get the most out of your equipment.

Desludging and Other Tank Maintenance

No matter how clean you keep your gutters or pipes or how well the openings on your tank are covered, it is inevitable that debris and sediment will make its way into your water tank. Over time, these materials will decompose in the tank to form a "sludge" that has to be removed in order to keep your water clean and usable. Sludge forms particularly quickly when there is a lot of dust or ash in the air, and if you allow this substance to build up in your tank, it can lead to the growth of harmful bacteria such as E. coli and campylobacter in your water. Needless to say, this can have serious consequences for you and your family's health. Sludge can also block your filters, pumps, and pipes, thereby damaging these components. There are professional services available for those who don't want to desludge their open tanks, but anyone can do it by following the steps below:

1. If there is any water left in the tank, drain it and put it to good use around your house and garden.
2. Alternatively, if you don't want to drain your tank and lose any of your harvested rainwater, you can insert a pipe through the tank's inlet and use it to pump out the sludge at the bottom.
3. If you have two tanks, use them in a series: The first tank can be used to catch the first rain, and the sediment buildup in this tank can be cleaned by draining its water into the other tank. This water can be used to irrigate any plants that will not be eaten.
4. Once your tank is empty, fill it with clean water using a hosepipe. It is preferable to use a high-pressure hose if you have one, as this will make it easier to loosen and remove sludge from the sides and bottom of the tank.
5. The clean water should be used to flush out any dirty water that remains in your RWH system.
6. Repeat the process until the water coming out of the tank's outlet is clear.

7. The bottom of the tank can also be swept and cleaned by hand once it has been emptied, or you can vacuum it using a suction hose.

8. Make sure to check any filters and other components used to treat your water, as these can also become contaminated by sludge. If necessary, these should also be cleaned.

9. There are also "self-cleaning tanks" available that use vacuums to suck out sludge and contaminated water. However, these can be expensive, and thus not accessible to everyone.

Sludge should ideally be removed at the end of summer, because this is the time when the water level in your tank is likely to be at its lowest. As mentioned before, the buildup of sludge can be slowed down by covering the opening of your tank, using leaf strainers, installing UV filters, and regularly cleaning your gutters and pipes. Using a first flush diverter to redirect the first water of the rainy season can also prevent debris from your roof from entering your water. Depending on how much debris enters your tank, it's best to inspect it every two to three years to see if there is sludge buildup. You can also determine if there is sludge in your tank by testing your water for harmful bacteria—this is discussed in more detail in Chapter 9.

When you do clean your tank, remember to stay safe: You'll have to work in a confined space that may contain a large amount of water, so make sure you take all the necessary precautions and that you have someone to keep an eye on you, if possible. Also keep in mind that water and electricity are a deadly combination—switch off your pump when working in your tank, and remember to pull the plug to make sure no electricity can flow into the water.

Most rainwater tanks have a lifetime of 25 years if they are maintained regularly. That being said, certain factors such as hail, wind, snow, or excessive sun can damage your tank over time. Furthermore, animals, insects, and birds can cause wear and tear that may not be obviously visible to you. Most RWH tanks will come with a guarantee, but this won't be the case if you're using something else as a rain barrel. However, even if your tank does have a guarantee, it's best to inspect its various parts regularly:

- Make sure the structure of its roof and sides are still intact, and that your tank is not in danger of collapsing.
- Any gaps and holes in your tank—as well as its covers and pipe fittings—should be repaired so that you can avoid losing water, creating sludge buildup, or allowing mosquitoes to breed in your tank.
- Regularly check on the tank's fasteners as tanks that fall over are a great source of injury—and even death.
- Remember to also keep an eye out for mosquito larvae and algae in your tank and to follow the steps in Chapter 7 if you find any.

- If any of your tanks have fallen out of use, drain them and remove them from your property or, alternatively, turn them upside down or cut them up. Empty tanks are ideal breeding sites for mosquitoes, and they don't need more than an inch of water to make your life miserable!

Pump Maintenance

Maintaining the pump of your RWH system can be expensive, but at the same time, not doing so will cost you even more. If you allow your maintenance to fall behind, the money needed to repair your pump can far exceed what it would've cost you to do regular maintenance on it. Furthermore, many RWH systems rely on water pumps to get the right water pressure—and if your pump fails, so will your means of getting water from your tank.

Pumps are intricate electrical systems, and therefore some of the problems you may encounter with them will require expert help. However, there are a few things you can do yourself to make sure your pump continues to work efficiently and doesn't become damaged:

- Pumps require large amounts of clean water to run smoothly, so if you're running out of water, be more careful about how you use your pump.
- Any unusual noises in a rainwater pump is a bad sign: If you hear anything you shouldn't, it's best to

pay more attention to your pump and to repair what has been broken.

- Like any electrical appliance, pumps should be sheltered from weather conditions in a well-drained area that is free of debris and dust.
- Do routine maintenance checks, or call in the help of an expert to do this for you. Most pumps will have manufacturer's specifications that you can follow if you're unsure how they should be inspected, cleaned, and maintained.

OTHER MAINTENANCE CONSIDERATIONS

Cold Weather

Frozen Water in Your Water Tank

Most—if not all—of your RWH system will be situated outside, which means it's exposed to the weather. If weather conditions are extreme, this may be a problem; but luckily, if you know what to look out for, you can take the necessary steps to avoid damage to your system!

RWH systems may be weatherproofed to some extent, but freezing weather conditions will still have an effect on them. Because water molecules expand when they freeze, ice will put pressure on the structural integrity of anything containing it, including pipes. When water inside a tank freezes, it can damage the pump, the plumbing, and possibly even the tank itself.

If your system has an underground tank, freezing temperatures are a slightly smaller problem as the tank is insulated by the ground surrounding it, and this helps keep the water at a relatively constant temperature. Furthermore, if the water does freeze, it will most likely be only the top layer. The same applies to pipes that have been buried below the frost line. On the other hand, aboveground tanks are at far bigger risk when the weather turns cold because they are not insulated by their environment.

The best way to avoid damage during colder times is to consider the possibility of frost when designing and installing your RWH system. If you're worried about freezing temperatures, consider the following when deciding what system will work best for you:

- Larger tanks are at lower risk of freezing over as smaller volumes of water freeze faster; therefore, your tank size is important, especially if you live in a colder climate.
- Round tanks have smaller surface areas than square or rectangular tanks, and therefore less heat escapes from them; so it is better to install a round tank, if possible.
- Plastic and metal tanks have a similar rate of heat loss, but plastic tanks are better able to withstand the expansion that is created when water does freeze. In contrast, metal tanks can crack more easily.

- As much as you don't want the water inside your tank to freeze, you don't want any water to freeze outside your tank, either. This can be prevented by avoiding tank covers that are flat—as water can accumulate on their surface—and instead opting for a cover that is sloped so that water can run off it before it freezes.

- Still-standing water has a much larger chance of freezing, so if you're worried about frost, you can move the water in your tank by jostling the tank itself a little or install an implement—such as an aerator—that will keep the water in the tank moving.

- As mentioned before, underground tanks have a far lower risk of freezing over—provided they have been installed below the frost line. It may therefore be best to design your RWH system in such a way that the tank is underground, if possible.

- Just as water is lost through cracks or leaks in your rainwater tank and all its associated pipes, heat also escapes through these openings. Thus, it's a good idea to inspect all the different components of your RWH system before the first frost arrives to make sure everything is sealed up tightly.

- When installing your pipes, make sure their angles are at the proper gradient so that water can't collect in them; this will not only protect your pipes from freezing, but will also lower the risk of bacteria and algae growing in stagnant water.

Many people who don't have to use their RWH systems during winter choose to drain them in order to prevent them from becoming damaged. This is known as "winterizing," and it can be done as follows:

1. Drain all water from your tank, unless you're completely sure it won't freeze.
2. Drain all of your pipes, and make sure there is no standing water in any part of your system.
3. Redirect the flow of rainwater so that it doesn't enter the tank, but instead flows straight into your downspout.
4. Cover the various parts of your system—such as your tank—as best you can.
5. If possible, remove the pump and store it in a safe, dry place.

While winterizing your system is an option, many of us may need to continue using our water tanks during winter, and therefore face the risks of colder temperatures. If you struggle with frost and frozen water, you can insulate your water tank by wrapping it in insulating blankets made of fiberglass, ceramic fiber, or mineral wool. You can also add aluminum sheets to the blankets to reflect heat back into the tank and to further protect your RWH system from cold temperatures. Insulating your RWH system is relatively easy, and you can do it yourself:

1. Measure the height and diameter of your tank to determine its surface area.

2. Determine the surface area of the top of the tank, and add it to the dimensions you calculated in step 1; this will tell you how much insulating material to buy. Remember, it's better to overestimate than to underestimate!

3. Once you have bought your insulation, wrap it around the sides of the tank as well as its top. The insulating material can be fastened with straps or other appropriate fasteners.

4. It's unnecessary to insulate the bottom of the tank, as heat rises and therefore only escapes from the sides and top of a barrel.

5. If possible, you can also insulate the pipes of your system, especially those that are most exposed. Remember that pipes will freeze even faster than the tank, so you have to pay attention to them, too.

6. Frozen pipes can also be prevented by lining them with heat strip tape, which is a type of tape that heats water using electricity. If you decide to use this, make sure you choose tape that turns on when the temperature drops below a certain level so that you can save as much electricity as possible.

7. Insulation requires very little maintenance, aside from occasionally checking if the blankets have become loosened or torn anywhere.

If you don't want to insulate your tank and you're willing to spend a little more money, it is possible to install a water heater to prevent water in your tank from freezing. There are several different types of water heaters available:

- A submersible water heater heats the water using an electric current and a heating element. These heaters are fairly simple and relatively cheap, but if the weather is very cold, you may require more than one heater or a combination of heaters and insulation.
- Electric heating blankets are wrapped around water tanks, and they combine the idea of insulation with water heating technology to prevent water from freezing. These blankets are available in different shapes and sizes, and often their temperature settings can be regulated so that you can set them to the exact temperature you want. However, they are a more expensive option and they require more maintenance than regular insulation blankets.
- Water tanks can also be heated from the outside using a machine that is installed underneath the tank. It's recommended that these systems only be used for very large RWH systems that are in very cold climates, as these machines are big and costly, and they require professional maintenance.
- It's possible to recirculate hot water into your RWH system by using a heat pump, and this will prevent water from freezing and damaging your system.

Other Components in Freezing Weather

Your RWH system will have different components depending on the specificities of its design, but here are some things that should be considered when the temperature starts to drop:

- Metal is more susceptible to damage than plastic when temperatures become freezing, and metal elements should therefore be exposed as little as possible.
- Control units should not be installed outside; instead, it's best to keep them indoors or in well-insulated and dry areas.
- Make sure your water pump is easily removable so that you can take it out of your RWH system if you decide to drain your system during winter.
- Backflow preventers are made of metal and therefore very sensitive to freezing conditions; it's best to drain these completely during winter to prevent them from cracking.
- UV equipment can be damaged by frost, so that equipment should be protected from frost.
- RWH filter collector units are not affected by freezing temperatures: They will simply stop collecting water if the water freezes, and start again once the water has thawed out.

Hot Weather

High temperatures aren't necessarily as big a problem as freezing weather, but too much heat and sun can still have a negative impact on your RWH system. For instance, excessive exposure to direct sunlight will degrade the various components faster—such as the tank and pipes—and they will have to be inspected and repaired more often. In addition, hot water promotes the growth of bacteria and algae; while this won't have a negative impact on your garden, you shouldn't use water in your house or on your crops if it wasn't shielded from the sun in one way or another.

Just like underground tanks are better insulated against the cold, the water stored in them will also be less affected by high temperatures. Additionally, water tanks can be insulated against the sun in the same way they would be protected against frost. A storage tank placed in the sun can become damaged, and the water in it becomes a breeding ground for algae and bacteria. It's therefore better to place your tank in the shade as far as possible, to prevent your water from becoming unusable.

HOW TO SCHEDULE YOUR MAINTENANCE

A RWH system requires quite a lot of maintenance, especially if your system is more complex. The good news is that you don't have to do it all at once—if you schedule your maintenance, you can spread the work out through the year while still making sure your system functions efficiently and safely.

Three Months

Your gutters, pipes, and roof have to be inspected and cleaned every three months. This is especially important at the end of the dry season just before the first rainfall, as this is the time when the most debris collects in your RWH system. Cleaning your roof and gutters includes removing any leaves, dust, pollen, droppings, twigs, or other organic matter, as well as trim back tree branches around your roof and gutters. If you find that these components get very dirty very quickly, you may have to consider cleaning them more often. For instance, if there are trees overhanging your roof or gutters, chances are there will be more debris in your RWH system that will have to be cleared out regularly.

In addition to cleaning your gutters, you also have to inspect your gutter mesh and leaf screens. In order to do this, make sure there are no holes or tears in the mesh, and that all screens are still fastened in place securely. If they have become clogged, you should remove the debris and replace them before the next rainfall event.

Six Months

It's important that you check the structural integrity of your pipes and gutters at least twice a year, as loose pipes can cause severe injuries and damage. When inspecting the safety of your pipes, make sure to check their fasteners too, as well as any places where there might be leakages.

As for your rainwater tank, it's important to inspect the water quality every six months, even if you don't use the water for potable uses such as cooking and drinking. In addition to mosquitoes and algae that can carry diseases into your water, other animals and insects may also occasionally find their way into your water tank. It's best to make sure they can't gain access to your water by inspecting the tank for any openings, and to clean your tank if you find any algae or mosquito larvae. When inspecting your tank, check the inside for any floating debris, flaking paint, corrosion, oily films, dust, and sludge, and clean and repair what is necessary.

In addition to the inside of your tank, it's also best to check the quality of your water, and to clean and replace your water filters where needed. Evaporation during the summer months can increase the buildup of sediment in your filters, and this can reduce their efficiency and lower the quality of your water. If you have a water pump, this should also be serviced every six months.

Yearly

If you want to get the most out of your RWH system, you have to inspect it fully every year. This includes checking the roof, gutters, pipes, and fittings, as well as the filters and pumps. It's also important to ensure that your tank is still structurally sound and that all its fasteners are in place to prevent it from falling over and causing damage.

Two to Three Years

Desludging a tank can be hard work, but fortunately, it only has to be done once every two to three years. No matter how clean your gutters, pipes, and roof are, it's likely that sludge will still find its way into your tank. In order to avoid using contaminated water in your house and on your crops, it's best to have this removed, even if it's a bit of a hassle. To desludge your tank effectively, follow the guidelines and advice earlier in this chapter.

After Heavy Rainfall Events

First flush diverters receive a lot of debris, so they should be cleaned after every three rainfall events. This can be done by cleaning the outlets and emptying the filters to prevent them from becoming blocked.

Safety Considerations

Harvesting rainwater is a wonderful way to prepare your family for possible water-related disasters in the future and to contribute to global sustainability. It's a practice that is becoming more and more popular, and RWH systems are becoming more safe and efficient by the day. That being said, there are still a few things you should be cautious of when using harvested rainwater in your home and garden:

- If you plan on drinking rainwater or using it for cooking, make sure it is filtered and treated first. Although rain is a fantastic resource, raindrops can pick up harmful substances in the air and on different surfaces, and carry it straight into your home.

- The same applies if you want to use rainwater to water your crops. While unfiltered water can be used for the rest of your garden, fruits, herbs, and vegetables should only be irrigated with treated water. If you want to put it in your body, the water has to be decontaminated first!

- It might be tempting, but using rainwater in your swimming pool is not a good idea. This is because rainwater—especially if it's been standing still for a long time—may contain bacteria, fungi, parasites, and viruses, all of which can have a negative impact on your skin, eyes, mouth, and other organs.

No matter how well they have been designed, RWH systems can be dangerous if they are not installed and maintained correctly. Make sure you avoid injury by considering the following:

- If you decide to install your system by yourself, make sure you follow any possible safety precautions. This may mean using personal protective equipment— such as gloves and safety glasses—and being careful

RAINWATER HARVESTING FOR YOUR HOMESTEAD | 161

when handling heavy objects. Furthermore, if your system comes with specific installation requirements, make sure you follow them.

- Rainwater tanks are big and heavy—especially when full—and if one of these were to fall on someone, it can cause serious injuries. To prevent this, make sure your tank is fastened in place securely.

- Unfortunately, rainwater tanks have been the cause of drowning-related accidents; so it's very important to make sure that tanks have lids or screens to cover them and that these are locked in place.

- The time will come when you have to clean your tank, and when you do, it's vital you make sure you do so safely. In addition to tank maintenance, also make sure you are cautious when cleaning gutters and pipes, especially if you are using a ladder.

Maintaining your tank is important, and so is staying safe while you're doing it. At the same time, you always have to know how to treat rainwater. Water is essential for life, but if your potable and non-potable water is not treated properly, it could make you and your family ill. The next chapter will teach you how to ensure your water is safe so that you can get the best out of your RWH system.

CHAPTER 9: WATER QUALITY AND TREATMENT

I n previous chapters, we talk about the quality of rainwater, and how this affects what it can be used for. It's been said before, but it is important enough to be repeated: Rainwater isn't necessarily fit to drink as it falls out of the sky. That being said, it doesn't mean it can't be made safe! In this chapter, we discuss how to analyze the quality and purity of your water, how you can determine what it can safely be used for, and ways that the water can be treated or purified to remove contaminants and make it potable. There are many ways to purify your water: Treatment and purification can be incorporated into the system itself, into the storage tank, or performed between the tank and use—we look into how this is done to determine which method suits your RWH system best, and how you can be sure that you've chosen the right one.

RAINWATER QUALITY AND CONTAMINATION CONCERNS

When we think of rain, we imagine something refreshing falling from the sky... but the reality is, rainwater can become contaminated. As a result of air pollution, there are harmful particles in the sky that can dissolve in falling rain and become part of our harvested water. In addition, the catchment area, conveyance system, and tank that rainwater comes into contact with as it travels through a RWH system can also pollute the water. There are some concerns about certain roofing materials—especially asphalt shingles—as some roofs, especially older ones, may contain asbestos and other harmful chemicals. Furthermore, debris, algae, and waterborne bacteria aren't the only concerns when it comes to contamination from your storage tank—harmful chemicals in the tank itself can also leach into the water. This is a particularly big problem with plastic barrels—especially when the water remains in there for a long time, or the plastic barrels are exposed to a lot of direct sunlight. The one chemical people are most worried about in this regard is bisphenol A—or BPA—because it can lead to increased blood pressure, heart conditions, and even type 2 diabetes. Hence, it's important to do enough research before you buy a storage tank—and it's just as important to treat your water to make sure it's of good quality before you use it.

But what is meant by "water quality?" Rainwater can be classified as "potable" or "non-potable." The first, potable, means it's drinkable and that it can be used for anything where it will be consumed—including cooking, washing dishes, washing fruit and vegetables, and bathing. The second, non-potable, refers to water that can't be consumed, and is therefore only fit for irrigation and other uses where it won't come into contact with people, such as fire protection, flushing toilets, and outdoor washing. The reason why this distinction exists is because potable water doesn't contain any harmful bacteria or contaminants while non-potable water may contain pollutants that can cause people to become ill. When it comes to irrigating edible crops, there is some debate about whether water should be potable or not. Some studies claim plants don't take up substances such as BPA through their roots, and therefore using non-potable water to irrigate them isn't a problem. On the other hand, people have also found that certain vegetables—in particular root crops—do take up BPA, and that this chemical can make its way into your home in this way. As for water contamination from air pollution, keep in mind that while this water isn't safe to drink, it can be used for irrigation—after all, it does sometimes rain directly on your plants, too!

There is no national legislation that governs water quality standards, but some states may have regulations that govern this aspect of RWH. When you start to think about purification, it's best to also keep this in mind. Typically, "water quality" is determined according to these factors:

- The acidity or alkalinity of the water is an important element in determining its safety, especially in areas where air pollution and "acid rain" is a problem. While the air quality has a big impact on the pH of rainwater, it can also be affected by the material your barrel is made of. For example, concrete tanks can make water slightly more alkaline due to the lime found in this material. Rainwater normally has a pH of about 5.7, although this will differ depending on the region.
- Water comes into contact with countless particles on its journey to your storage tank, and the nature of these particles play an important role in determining the quality of your water. Debris and sludge make up the most prominent part of particulate matter, but things such as dust, smoke, soot, vehicle exhaust

fumes, and agricultural and industrial emissions can all make their way into rainwater.

- The final determining factor of the quality of water is the chemical compounds found in it. There are an endless number of chemicals that can contaminate water, but some of their most common sources are fertilizer residue in the air and industrial emissions.

- Your catchment area has an enormous impact on the quality of your water, and certain roofing materials can cause more harm than good by contaminating your rainwater to such an extent that it becomes unusable. Debris that collects on roofs also impacts the quality of your water, which is why it's important to install the necessary filters to prevent this matter from getting into your tank.

- Unfortunately, rainwater tanks themselves can also be a source of contamination, and chemicals from unsafe or unlined rain barrels can leach into your water. Furthermore, the sludge that builds up over time at the bottom of your tank can become disturbed and pollute your water, especially if your tank isn't well-maintained.

- As mentioned in Chapter 7, algae and mosquitoes are dangerous sources of contamination, and they can introduce a range of diseases and viruses to your water.

DIFFERENT TYPES OF FILTRATION AND WATER TREATMENT

Potable and non-potable water goes through different treatment processes, and there are various levels of filtration. Therefore, before you choose a purification system, you first have to decide how and where you want to use your harvested rainwater. Furthermore, water can also be treated at different places in the RWH system: Some methods, such as screens, are "point-of-entry" treatment methods. This means they purify water at the point where it enters the storage tank. Other methods—in particular those that kill microorganisms—are "point-of-use" forms of purification, which means it's something you'll do after you've captured your rainwater, but before you use it. Since each treatment method serves a different purpose, it's possible to combine various purification systems to get the best quality water you possibly can.

Algae, bacteria, mosquitoes, and debris from catchment areas and conveyance systems are all possible sources of contamination. Therefore, your first step of action should be to minimize or avoid the contamination caused by them. There are many strategies throughout this book that tell you how you can design a safe RWH system, and some of these include having an opaque tank that is kept out of the sun, using mesh to keep out mosquitoes, and installing screens and a first flush diverter to keep your tank clean of debris. A further contaminant is the sludge that builds up in the bottom of your tank. In this regard, tank mainte-nance is very important. Additionally, you can also "calm" the water so that the sludge is disturbed as little as possible.

If you find your water still has larger particles and debris in it when you remove it from the tank, or if some of the sludge or sediment in the tank has mixed with the water, you can filter it through a finer mesh to remove these particles. These devices are known as "particulate filters," and the finer the mesh they have, the smaller the particles it will remove. At the same time, finer mesh will also become blocked more easily. These filtration devices are graded according to the minimum size of particles they can remove, and some of them can remove smaller than 0.5 mm. Additionally, it's also possible to buy self-cleaning filters that require little maintenance.

For advanced filtration, you can always turn to UV filters. These devices use ultraviolet light to kill living microorganisms in the water, which means it's unlikely that any bacteria or other pathogens will make its way into your home. Keep in mind that a UV filter doesn't remove fine particles from the water, so your rainwater will still have to be run through a particulate filter to make sure it's free of sediment. These larger particles in the water can also "shade" organisms and protect them from the UV light, so it's best to remove any particles before you use UV filtration.

In addition to UV filtration, there are also other ways to get rid of microorganisms in water. The first is boiling water before it's used. Unfortunately, this method is time-consuming and it uses a lot of electricity, and is therefore only efficient when small quantities of water is needed. Water can also be treated chemically with chlorine or bleach, provided these are used in the right quantities. Additionally, in order to remove these substances from your water once they have killed living pathogens, water can be run through a carbon filter. Using this type of filtration will also improve the taste of the water, because it removes the particles that cause odors and unpleasant tastes.

More complex methods of filtration include nanofiltration, which is a process that uses a membrane with a very small pore size to purify water. Water can also be purified through reverse osmosis by pushing it through a semipermeable membrane using extreme pressure, or by treating it with ozone gas during the process of ozonation. There are many types of filters and devices available, and oftentimes budget will be a big deciding factor when these choices have to be made. While it's important not to spend unnecessary money on a water treatment device or method, it's impossible to put a price on safety—especially when it comes to the safety of your water.

TESTING YOUR WATER

It's important to purify potable water—but how will you know if your treatment methods are working? Aside from showing physical symptoms of illness, you most likely won't know if your water is safe to drink unless you test it. In order to make sure your equipment is working, it's helpful to test it before and after it's been treated; this will help you detect any changes—or lack thereof—and therefore determine the safety of your water. Water should also be tested regularly in order to make sure your purification system is still functioning effectively.

When testing water, there are two things you can test for: The first is the pH of the water, which will help you establish if your water is too acidic to be used in your household. The second is the presence of pathogens and microorganisms, as well as harmful chemicals. There are many home-testing kits available for water, which saves you the time and trouble of having to send water to expensive laboratories.

At last—you have designed your RWH system, and you know how to maintain it and keep your water safe... now, all that's left to learn is how you can use the rainwater you've collected in your homestead!

CHAPTER 10: APPLICATIONS FOR HARVESTED RAINWATER

I n previous chapters, we've discussed a number of things you can do with harvested rainwater—everything from flushing the toilet, to irrigating crops, to filling a pond for ducks, to washing your car and farm equipment! In this chapter, we're going to delve deeper into common uses for rainwater, and what you can do to make sure your system is properly set up for what you want to do with the water you collect. We'll also touch on water purity, when you have to be concerned about it, and when the rainwater is safe to use as is.

RAINWATER HARVESTING

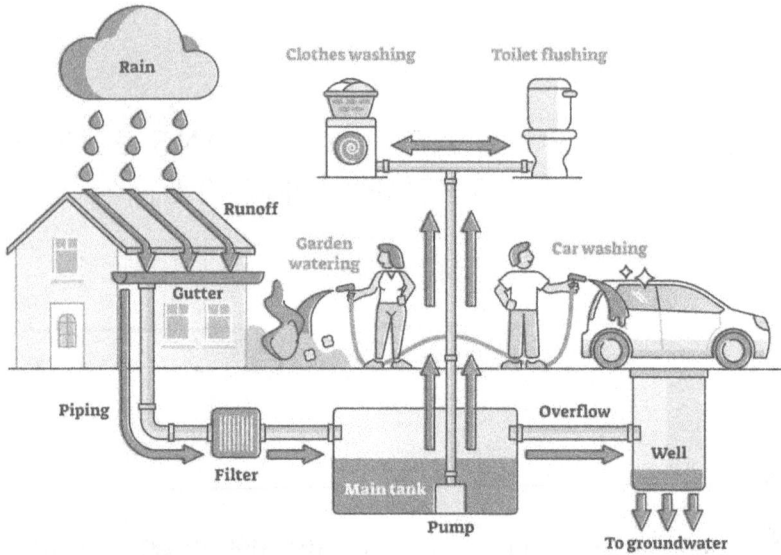

USING RAINWATER IN THE GARDEN AND BEYOND

Rainwater isn't really fit for consumption when it falls out of the sky—though with some purification, people do safely use it for drinking, cooking, or bathing. However, if you don't want to invest in a purification system, that doesn't mean RWH is useless to you. There are plenty of things to use rainwater for that don't require it.

Rainwater in Your House

Ideally, rainwater can be used for drinking, cooking, washing produce, bathing, indoor cleaning, laundry, and washing dishes. However, all of these functions involve putting water on or in your body, and therefore a little more care needs to be taken to avoid getting sick. While rainwater is free of some contaminants you might find in lakes or rivers, it's not necessarily safe to drink. Instead, it has to be purified in order to be made safe to use for the functions above. Purification removes particulate contaminants and kills off dangerous bacteria; this is discussed in more detail in Chapter 9.

Flushing Toilets

If you have a pump system attached to the storage tank your RWH system sends water to, you can set it up so that this is the water that fills the toilet bowl. This is an ideal use for rainwater, because there's no need for your toilet water to be potable—nobody's drinking it (except perhaps a misbehaving dog!).

Watering Livestock and Irrigating Crops

Using rainwater for crops and livestock is probably one of its most common applications. Unlike humans, animals don't necessarily need their drinking water to be purified—how would they survive in the wild otherwise? Likewise, your outdoor plants will be perfectly happy to be irrigated with rainwater, and you can even use a clever system to divert the rain straight to them.

There are many options if you want to use rainwater in your garden. For instance, if you want to keep it simple, you can manually attach a hosepipe to your tank or use its spigot to fill a watering can, and use this water to irrigate your crops. If you have a very big garden, want to save time, or your tank does not have enough pressure, you can install a pump to divert water into an irrigation system that you can turn on whenever necessary. Keep in mind that pumps and irrigation systems tend to use more water, and if you have a small rainwater tank, it's likely this type of system will empty it quite quickly.

Rainwater is ideal for plants, because unlike municipal water, it doesn't contain any chlorine. While it may be unsafe for us to drink, most plants love the slight acidity of rainwater—and your garden will thank you for this treat! At the same time, you should take care when watering edible crops with rainwater. While the crops themselves won't be harmed, bacteria in the water can be transferred to them—and to you —if you're not careful about using only safe and treated water in this section of your garden. If you absolutely have to use your rainwater to irrigate your crops, make sure to spray the water as close to the ground as possible so that none of it splashes onto the leaves and stems of the plants themselves.

Outdoor Washing

If you don't have a water purification system, fear not—you can wash your car, farm equipment, pavement, or anything else on your property with harvested rainwater without worrying about contaminants getting into your living space, drinking water, or food.

Fire Protection

If you have an underground storage tank with a pump, harvested rainwater is the ideal thing to drown an unexpected fire. Although water used in fire protection systems doesn't have to be safe to drink, there are nevertheless certain quality controls that the water must pass. This is to ensure that the rainwater won't corrode the fire system or clog any of the fire pumps. In addition, there may also be requirements as to how much water you must store at a time for this use, and how often the tank must be inspected. These requirements are likely to depend on local regulations, so make sure you take a look at them before you create this sort of system at your house.

Pools and Ponds

If you're going to have tons of water just sitting around your property, why not give yourself some luxury and use it to fill a pool or pond? For example, swimming pools are a fine use of rainwater, and you can even divert water directly into them. Just add chlorine, make sure you don't drink it by accident, and cover it when not in use to make sure mosquitoes don't start breeding in it.

Likewise, if you keep ducks or another type of water bird, it's best for them to have water to paddle in. Some people even build entire ponds for this purpose... and rainwater is the perfect thing to fill it with. If you're interested in creating a permaculture-style RWH system such as those described in Chapter 3, you can also "stack functions" with a pond—by planting crops that need to be in water or even stocking the pond with fish. If you have the space, you can even install water features in your garden, and use the rainwater from your tank to feed them.

LEAVE A REVIEW

A quick message before we start the conclusion of this book. If you're enjoying this book, I'd kindly like to ask you to leave a brief review on Amazon. Reviews aren't easy to come by, but they have a profound impact. So I would be incredibly thankful if you could just take a minute to leave a quick review on the Amazon review page, even if it's just a sentence or two!

To do so, just scan the QR Code or click the link below. This will take you to the "rate and review" page where you can enter your star rating and then write a sentence or two about the book. It's that simple! Again, just scan the QR Code or click the link below. Enter your star rating and that's it!

Please click this link to leave a review on Amazon!

https://amazon.com/review/create-review?&asin= B0BPD22BG2

https://www.facebook.com/Hayden.A.Warner/

Thank you so much for taking the time to leave a short review on Amazon. I am very appreciative as your review makes a difference. Now back to your scheduled programming.

CONCLUSION

Water is becoming increasingly scarce, and yet, we as a human race can't live without it. With changing weather patterns and encroaching deserts, our risk of running out of water is becoming greater every day... luckily, we have been blessed with a wonderful resource right above our heads— the rain! Using rainwater in your house and garden is not only free, it can also be easy and affordable—if you know how. Furthermore, it reduces pressure on municipal infrastructure, prevents flooding and erosion, and saves you and your family money.

There is nothing more satisfying than living a sustainable life, but it doesn't come without a little bit of research. If you are new to the world of RWH, it's best to first find out if there are any regulations in your area that govern this practice, and how these will influence your plans. Next, you should understand the principles that underlie permaculture and RWH so that you can build a system that is self-sufficient and easy to maintain.

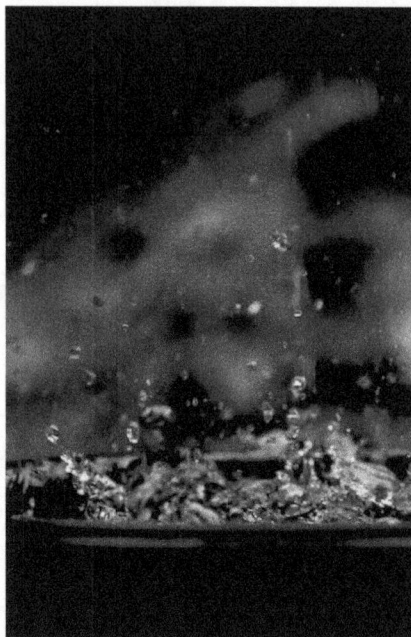

For those of you who thought RWH was only limited to water tanks and gutters, think again! There are many things you can do in your landscape to collect rainwater and help your garden flourish. However, if you want to go further, it's possible to design, build, and install your own RWH system —all that's needed is an understanding of the components of a RWH system, how your site works, what your needs are, and how you can create the system that best incorporates all of these aspects.

Once you've installed your RWH system, your work hasn't ended yet. No matter how well you've planned it, there are always things that can go wrong. Luckily, many have done this before you, and there are a few common mistakes that can easily be avoided if you know what to look out for. Depending on what you want to use your water for, you also have to make sure it's safe by testing, filtering, and purifying it… and once you've taken care of business, you can, at last, start reaping the benefits of your RWH system!

RWH is an ongoing process that you'll have to keep maintaining and improving on your system as you learn more. Not only will your environment change, but so will your needs, and it's important to keep adjusting and adapting your system as necessary. Nevertheless, it's worthwhile—rain is the gift that keeps on giving.

ABOUT THE AUTHOR

Hayden Warner is a third-generation homesteader who has dedicated his life to promote the sustainable ways of living imparted to him by his family—especially when it comes to how we use our natural resources. He is particularly passionate about rain, as it's a valuable freshwater resource that normally goes untapped. By learning to utilize it, he has realized water security in his own life—he now has a dependable water source that has recharged various natural resources around his property and that also takes care of his own domestic water needs. In addition to living sustainably, Hayden also wants to share his knowledge with others to make sure his readers can find independence by collecting and harvesting rainwater in their own lives.

GLOSSARY

Barrage: A type of dam that has several gates through which water can be let out.

Berm: The strip of land that borders a swale; a berm can either be raised or flat.

Cistern: A tank, barrel, or reservoir used to store water.

Collection area: Also known as a catchment area—the surface area from which rainwater is harvested.

Conveyance system: The collection of pipes, gutters, downspouts, and conduits that transfers water through a RWH system from the catchment area to the storage tank, as well as from the tank to the water's final destination.

Desludging: The process of removing sludge from the bottom of a storage tank.

Frost line: The depth to which moisture in the soil freezes; also known as frost depth.

Gabion: A type of dam that is constructed with a permeable material so that water can still move through it, although at a much slower rate.

Groundcover: Densely planted vegetation that often has small, fine roots that holds the soil together and covers the ground entirely.

Leaf-strainer: A coarse mesh that is installed in gutters and downspouts and over the opening of rainwater storage tanks used to prevent debris from entering these tanks; also known as leaf screens.

Overflow: Any surplus rainwater that can't be accommodated in the storage tank; can also refer to the "overflow system," which is the system that has been put in place to make sure extra rainwater doesn't go to waste.

Permaculture: The practice of developing self-sufficient and sustainable agricultural ecosystems.

Sludge: The mixture of solid and liquid decomposed organic matter that collects at the bottom of a storage tank over time.

Spigot: A tap or valve that is used to let rainwater out of a storage tank.

Swales: Ditches or trenches that are dug along contour lines to divert rainwater in a certain direction, and to slow it down so that it can seep into the ground.

Terrace: An earthen structure that intercepts and reduces the rate of runoff on moderate to steep slopes, to allow soil particles to settle.

REFERENCES

American Water Works Association. (2009). *Planning for the distribution of reclaimed water: Manual of water supply practices* (3rd ed.). American Water Works Association.

APEC Water Systems. (n.d.). *How mosquitoes affect the quality of your water.* Freedrinkingwater.com. https://www.freedrinkingwater.com/water_health/health1/1-mosquitoes-effects-on-water.htm

Arizona High Desert Gardening. (2018, October 4). *Rain barrel spigot comparison and DIY* [Video]. YouTube. https://www.youtube.com/watch?v=5UY7j6vt_yk

Arnot, J. (2020, September 2). *How & why does algae grow in a water storage tank?* Enduraplas. https://blog.enduraplas.com/water-storage-rain-harvesting/how-why-does-algae-grow-in-a-water-storage-tank

Barnes, D. (2014, May 31). *6 tips for water-harvesting earthworks.* Permaculture Reflections; EcoEdge Design Ltd. https://www.permaculturereflections.com/6-tips-for-water-harvesting-earthworks/

Battenberg, G.E. (2009, September 14). *Flowing issues: A brief history of rainwater harvesting.* Water Conditioning and Purification International. https://wcponline.com/2009/09/14/flowing-issues-brief-history-rainwater-harvesting/

Bauer, B. A. (2022, March 8). *What is BPA, and what are the concerns about BPA?* Mayo Clinic. https://www.mayoclinic.org/healthy-lifestyle/nutrition-and-healthy-eating/expert-answers/bpa/faq-20058331

Bioenergy Education Initiative. (n.d.). *Growing algae for fuel.* Oregon State University. https://agsci.oregonstate.edu/sites/agscid7/files/bioenergy/education/algae_final_interactive.pdf

Blue Mountain Co. (n.d.). *Rain harvesting maintenance checklist.* Blue Mountain Co. https://rainharvesting.com.au/wp-content/uploads/sites/2/2018/10/Rain-Harvesting-Maintenance-Checklist.pdf

Blue Mountain Co. (2017a, September). *Mosquito prevention in rain harvesting systems.* Rain Harvesting; Blue Mountain Co. https://rainharvesting.com.

au/field-notes/articles/rain-harvesting/mosquito-prevention-in-rain-harvesting-systems/

Blue Mountain Co. (2017b, September). *Why use first flush diverters?* Rain Harvesting; Blue Mountain Co. https://rainharvesting.com.au/field-notes/articles/rain-harvesting/the-benefits-of-using-first-flush-diverters/

BrainyQuote.com. (n.d.). *Jacques Yves Cousteau quotes.* BrainyQuote.com; BrainyMedia Inc. https://www.brainyquote.com/quotes/jacques_yves_cousteau_204405

Brand, R. (2014, June 21). *Mosquitofish - the care, feeding and breeding of mosquitofish (Mosquito fish).* Aquarium Tidings. https://aquariumtidings.com/mosquitofish/

Bussey, A. (2022, June 20). *How to calculate gutter slope.* Blue River Gutters. https://blueivergutters.com/how-to-calculate-gutter-slope/

Castelo, J. (2021, December 13). *How to select the best rain barrel pump for your system.* World Water Reserve. https://worldwaterreserve.com/rain-barrel-pump/

Clayton, B., Kniffen, B., & Woodson, D. (n.d.). *Making a rain barrel.* AgriLife Extension: Texas A&M Service. https://www.harvesth2o.com/adobe_files/Making%20a%20Rainbarrel%20-%20AgriLife%20Extension.pdf

Coerco Agriculture. (2018, July 19). *Cleaning sludge out of your water tank.* Coerco Agriculture. https://agriculture.coerco.com.au/agriculture-blog/cleaning-sludge-water-tank

Cowie, A. (2018, October 26). *Ancient rainwater harvesting: It fell from the sky and became worshiped by every civilization.* Ancient Origins. https://www.ancient-origins.net/history-ancient-traditions/ancient-rainwater-harvesting-0010904%20/

Crosbie, D. (2022, March 5). *Rainwater collection laws (Legalities explained).* Climatebiz. https://climatebiz.com/rainwater-collection-laws/

Daily, C., & Wilkins, C. (2012). *Passive water harvesting: Rainwater collection.* The University of Arizona College of Agriculture and Life Sciences.

Dallman, S., Chaudhry, A. M., Muleta, M. K., & Lee, J. (2016). The value of rain: Benefit-cost analysis of rainwater harvesting systems. *Water Resources Management,* *30*(12), 4415–4428. https://doi.org/10.1007/s11269-016-1429-0

Daniel, A. (2018, November 16). *This is why it's illegal to collect rainwater in some states*. Best Life. https://bestlifeonline.com/illegal-collect-rainwater/

David The Good. (2016, December 5). *Top 7 mistakes to avoid when harvesting rainwater* [Video]. YouTube. https://www.youtube.com/watch?v=zxcthuHEXUY

Drevets, T. (2021, May 20). *10 mistakes to avoid when harvesting rainwater*. Homestead Survival Site. https://homesteadsurvivalsite.com/mistakes-avoid-harvesting-rain-water/

Dyer, M. H. (2021, January 4). *Mosquito control in rain barrels: How to control mosquitoes in a rain barrel*. Gardening Know How. https://www.gardeningknowhow.com/plant-problems/pests/insects/mosquito-control-in-rain-barrels.htm

Eccles, A. (2018, November 24). *Home rainfall collection calculator*. National Tank Outlet. https://www.ntotank.com/blog/home-rainfall-collection-calculator

Eliades, A. (2010, January 22). *How to make a rainwater tank from recycled plastic drums*. Deep Green Permaculture. https://deepgreenpermaculture.com/2010/01/22/recycled-plastic-drum-rainwater-tank/

Enduraplas. (2019, May 1). *3 ways to eliminate algae growth in water tanks [Guaranteed]*. [Video]. YouTube. https://www.youtube.com/watch?v=GaLiYCaHq4Y

Eslamian, S., & Eslamian, F. (2021, March 1). *Handbook of water harvesting and conservation: Basic concepts and fundamentals* (1st ed.). John Wiley & Sons, Inc.

Evans, M. (2019, December 1). *How to design a rainwater harvesting system*. LiveAbout. https://www.thebalancesmb.com/design-a-rainwater-harvesting-system-in-6-steps-3157815

Constrofacilitator. (2021, August 5). *Rainwater harvesting; advantages, types and methods*. Constrofacilitator. https://www.constrofacilitator.com/rainwater-harvesting-advantages-types-and-methods/

Fant, M. O. (2019a, June 4). *Rainwater harvesting: Surveying*. Santa Cruz Permaculture. https://santacruzpermaculture.com/2019/06/surveying/

Fant, M. O. (2019b, August 12). *Rainwater harvesting: Berms and swales*. Santa Cruz Permaculture. https://santacruzpermaculture.com/2019/08/berms-swales/

Fant, M. O. (2021, January 28). *Rainwater harvesting: Brush check dams and gabions*. Santa Cruz Permaculture. https://santacruzpermaculture.com/2021/01/brush-check-dams-gabions/

Firth, C. (2017, March 10). *5 components every rainwater harvesting system must include*. Enduraplas. https://blog.enduraplas.com/water-storage-rain-harvesting/5-components-every-rainwater-harvesting-system-must-include

GoTo Tanks. (2019, November 21). *How to keep the water in a plastic storage tank from freezing*. GoTo Tanks. https://gototanks.com/plastic-storage-tanks/how-to-keep-the-water-in-a-plastic-storage-tank-from-freezing.html

Grant, B. L. (2021, March 25). *What is a swale: Learn about swales in the garden*. Gardening Know How. https://www.gardeningknowhow.com/garden-how-to/projects/swales-in-the-garden.htm

Guppy Aquarium. (2017, May 24). *Mosquitofish care guide*. GuppyAquarium.com. https://guppyaquarium.com/mosquitofish-care-guide/

Hall, B. M.. (2020, November 17). *3 common mistakes with rainwater harvesting (And how to avoid them!)*. Shades of Green Permaculture. https://shadesofgreenpermaculture.com/blog/techniques/3-common-mistakes-with-rainwater-harvesting/

Harvesting Aqua. (2020, September 2). *How to choose the best rainwater barrel spigot*. Harvesting Aqua. https://harvestingaqua.com/how-to-choose-rain-barrel-spigot/

Heusinkveld, D. (2022, July 28). *Harvesting the rain part 1: Passive rainwater harvesting*. Arizona Daily Star. https://tucson.com/lifestyles/harvesting-the-rain-part-1-passive-rainwater-harvesting/article_bf86a31e-4ac5-11eb-abd5-ff9729f748fb.html

Holm, B. A., Feehan, K. A., Shelton, D. P., Rodie, S. N., & Franti, T. G. (2014). Stormwater management: How to make a rain barrel. In *Extension Publications* (pp. 1–8). University of Nebraska: Lincoln Extension. https://extensionpublications.unl.edu/assets/pdf/ec2001.pdf

Homestead and Chill. (2019, December 5). *Rainwater collection systems 101 & FAQs*. Homestead and Chill. https://homesteadandchill.com/rainwater-collection-systems-101/

Homestead Launch. (n.d.). *Homestead water sources: Flowing water, wells, ponds, rainwater harvesting and more*. Homestead Launch. https://homesteadlaunch.com/water-sources/

How to prevent algae from growing in your water tank. (2017, December 18). Rainwater Tanks Direct. https://rainwatertanksdirect.com.au/blogs/prevent-algae-growing-water-tank/

Hunt, B., & Gee, K. (2021, March 31). *Mosquito control for rainwater harvesting systems.* NC State Extension; NC State Extension Publications. https://content.ces.ncsu.edu/mosquito-control-for-rainwater-harvesting-systems

Jebamalar, A., Ravikumar, G., & Meiyappan, G. (2012, February 16). Ground-water storage through rain water harvesting (RWH). *Clean - Soil, Air, Water, 40*(6), 1–6. https://doi.org/10.1002/clen.201100517

Jenkins, E. (2020, October 5). *7 ways to harvest rainwater for your (permaculture) garden.* New Life on a Homestead. https://www.newlifeonahomestead.com/harvest-rainwater-for-your-permaculture-garden/

Johnson, S. (2022, June 15). *How to get rid of algae in ponds.* WikiHow. https://www.wikihow.com/Get-Rid-of-Algae-in-Ponds

Johnson, S., & Madden, H. (2022, June 17). *7 ways to prevent algae in rain barrels.* WikiHow. https://www.wikihow.com/Prevent-Algae-in-Rain-Barrels

Jones, M. P., & Hunt, W. F. (2006). *Urban waterways: Choosing a pump for rainwater harvesting.* North Carolina Cooperative Extension Service. https://www.ctahr.hawaii.edu/hawaiirain/Library/Guides&Manuals/NC_Choosing-a-Pump4RWH2006.pdf

Lancaster, B. (n.d.). *Passive water harvesting.* Rainwater Harvesting for Drylands and Beyond. https://www.harvestingrainwater.com/water-harvesting/water-harvesting-principles/passive-water-harvesting/

Law, J. (2019, September). *How to budge the sludge in your water tank.* NSW Farmers. https://nswfarmers.org.au/NSWFA/Posts/The_Farmer/Tools/How_to_budge_the_sludge_in_your_water_tank.aspx

Lewis, P. (2013, December 22). Homestead water. *Backwoods Home Magazine.* https://www.backwoodshome.com/homestead-water/

Liaw, C.-H., & Tsai, Y.-L. (2007, June 8). Optimum storage volume of rooftop rainwater harvesting systems for domestic use. *Journal of the American Water Resources Association, 40*(4), 901–912. https://doi.org/10.1111/j.1752-1688.2004.tb01054.x

Lindholm, H. (2020, February 20). *Cleaning your rainwater tank.* Bushman Tanks. https://www.bushmantanks.com.au/blog/cleaning-your-rainwater-tank/

Lynda. (2013, June 14). *Small scale garden swale*. Lawn to Food. https://lawnto food.com/2013/06/small-scale-garden-swale/

Martinson, D. B., Ranatunga, N. U. K., & Gunaratne, A. M. C. H. A. (2002, January). Reducing rainwater harvesting system cost. *28th WEDC Conference*. 28th WEDC Conference, India.

Maxwell-Gaines, C. (2016, February 10). *What is rainwater harvesting?* Innovative Water Solutions LLC. https://www.watercache.com/faqs/rainwater-harvesting-defined

Minnesota Stormwater Manual. (2022, July 18). *Definitions for stormwater and rainwater harvest and use/reuse*. Minnesota Stormwater Manual; Minnesota Pollution Control Agency. https://stormwater.pca.state.mn.us/index.php/Definitions_for_stormwater_and_rainwater_harvest_and_use/reuse

Mishra, G.. (n.d.). *Components of rainwater harvesting systems and their uses*. The Constructor. https://theconstructor.org/water-resources/rainwater-harvesting-components/6739/

Orpheus. (2013, February 26). *Rainwater harvesting regulations state by state*. https://www.enlight-inc.com/blog/rainwater-harvesting-regulations-state-by-state/

Oweis, T. Y., Prinz, D., & Hachum, A. Y. (2012). *Water harvesting for agriculture in the dry areas*. Experimental Agriculture 40(1), 149. https://doi.org/10.1017/S0014479712000828

PASLR. (2022a). *Handy tips - DIY Pump maintenance*. PASLR. https://www.paslr.co.nz/technical-pumps/diy-pump-maintenance/

Pelmont, J. (2021, July 7). *5 mistakes everyone makes conserving rainwater*. Dave's Garden. https://davesgarden.com/guides/articles/5-mistakes-everyone-makes-conserving-rainwater

Pioneer Water Tanks. (n.d.). Using rainwater for fire protection, with regards to NFPA 13 A.23.21. In *Pioneer Water Tanks America*. https://pioneerwater tanksamerica.com/wp-content/uploads/2019/06/Using-Rainwater-for-Fire-Protection-with-Regards-to-NFPA-13-A.23.21-1.pdf

Pioneer Water Tanks. (n.d.). *Is collecting rainwater illegal in California?* Pioneer Water Tanks. https://pioneerwatertanks.com.au/is-collecting-rainwater-illegal-in-california-ca/

Pushard, D. (n.d.-a). *Comparing rainwater storage options*. HarvestH2O. https://www.harvesth2o.com/rainwaterstorage.shtml

Pushard, D. (n.d.-b). *Conveyance - Simple or complex.* HarvestH2O. https://www.harvesth2o.com/conveyance.shtml

Pushard, D. (n.d.-c). *Protect your rainwater system.* HarvestH2O. https://www.harvesth2o.com/freezing-rwh-system-components.shtml

Rainfill Tanks & Curved Roofing Supplies. (2017, September 15). *Protecting your rainwater tank from mosquitoes.* Rainfill Tanks and Curved Roofing Supplies. https://www.rainfilltanks.com.au/protecting-rainwater-tank-mosquitoes/

RainHarvest Systems. (2013, November 13). *A glossary of rainwater and greywater recycling terms.* The Watershed. https://www.rainharvest.com/blog/?p=137

Rainharvesting Systems. (n.d.-a). *Can rainwater harvesting be affected by extreme weather?* Rainharvesting Systems. https://rainharvesting.co.uk/can-rainwater-harvesting-be-affected-by-extreme-weather/

Rainharvesting Systems. (n.d.-b). *Servicing & maintenance of rainwater harvesting systems.* Rainharvesting Systems. https://rainharvesting.co.uk/servicing-maintenance-rainwater-harvesting-systems/

Rainharvesting Systems. (n.d.-c). *What are the main components of a rainwater harvesting system?* Rainharvesting Systems. https://rainharvesting.co.uk/what-are-the-main-components-of-a-rainwater-harvesting-system/

Rainharvesting Systems. (n.d.-d). *What is rainwater harvesting?* Rainharvesting Systems. https://rainharvesting.co.uk/what-is-rainwater-harvesting/

Rainharvesting Systems. (n.d.-e). *Four tips on how to purify rainwater: Where you need to start.* Rainharvesting Systems. https://rainharvesting.co.uk/4-tips-on-how-to-purify-rainwater-where-you-need-to-start/

RainWatch Filter. (n.d.). *RainWatch's rainwater tank filter system maintenance tips.* RainWatch. https://rainwatch.com.au/rainwater-tank-filter-system-maintenance/

Rainwater Management Solutions. (2018, March 1). *Rainwater harvesting 101: Pump selection.* Rainwater Management Solutions. https://rainwatermanagement.com/blogs/news/rainwater-harvesting-101-pump-selection

Rainwater tanks: A maintenance checklist for long-term benefits (2019, May 30). Coerco Agriculture. https://agriculture.coerco.com.au/agriculture-blog/rainwater-tanks-a-maintenance-checklist-for-long-term-benefits

Reaney, H. (2022, April 29). *Rainwater harvesting - save money with these sustain-*

able ideas. Homes & Gardens. https://www.homesandgardens.com/advice/rainwater-harvesting

Rainwater harvesting - Best practices guidebook. (2012, September). Regional District of Nanaimo. https://www.rdn.bc.ca/cms/wpattachments/wpID2430atID5059.pdf

Rinkesh, K.. (n.d.-a). *Rainwater harvesting: Advantages, disadvantages, uses and techniques.* Conserve Energy Future. https://www.conserve-energy-future.com/advantages_disadvantages_rainwater_harvesting.php

Rinkesh, K. (n.d.-b). *What is rainwater harvesting? Rainwater harvesting methods and techniques.* Conserve Energy Future. https://www.conserve-energy-future.com/methods-of-rainwater-harvesting.php

Roberts, T. (2017, August 1). *Storing water in the landscape: A swales and ponds primer.* Permaculture Research Institute. https://www.permaculturenews.org/2017/08/01/storing-water-landscape-swales-ponds-primer/

Rochat, E. (2018a, August 4). *Rainwater harvesting laws you need to know about.* Perfect Water. https://4perfectwater.com/blog/rainwater-harvesting-laws

Rochat, E. (2018b, August 23). *Roof types for rainwater harvesting.* Perfect Water. https://4perfectwater.com/blog/rainwater-harvesting-roof-types

Rochat, E. (2018c, July 3). *The history of rainwater harvesting.* Perfect Water. https://4perfectwater.com/blog/history-of-rainwater-harvesting

Savou, J. (2017, May 23). *To first flush, or not to first flush.* BlueBarrel Rainwater Catchment Systems. https://www.bluebarrelsystems.com/blog/first-flush-diverter/

Sepehri, M., Malekinezhad, H., Ilderomi, A. R., Talebi, A., & Hosseini, S. Z. (2018). Studying the effect of rain water harvesting from roof surfaces on runoff and household consumption reduction. *Sustainable Cities and Society, 43,* 317–324. https://doi.org/10.1016/j.scs.2018.09.005

Sevenson, T. (2015, March 17). *How to do rain water tank cleaning and maintenance, some basic tips.* Southern's Water Technology. https://southernswater.com.au/rain-water-tank-cleaning-maintenance-basic-tips/

Simply Starry Sustainable Living With God. (2017, June 10). *Top 7 mistakes to avoid when harvesting rainwater* [Video]. YouTube. https://www.youtube.com/watch?v=fBc8uDw_vNw

Singh, S., Samaddar, A. B., Srivastava, R. K., & Pandey, H. K. (2014). Groundwater recharge in urban areas: Experience of rain water harvesting.

Journal of the Geological Society of India, 83(6), 295–302. https://doi.org/10. 1007/s12594-014-0105-3

Stross, A. (2022a, June 15). *Here's a quick way to terrace a hill.* Tenth Acre Farm: Permaculture for the Suburbs. https://www.tenthacrefarm.com/quick-terrace-hill/

Stross, A. (2022b, June 15). *How to build a swale in the residential landscape.* Tenth Acre Farm: Permaculture for the Suburbs. https://www.tenthacre farm.com/how-to-build-swale/

Tetra Pond. (n.d.). *How to control algae and green water in your pond.* Tetra Pond. https://www.tetra-fish.com/pond/learning-center/get-educated/how-to-control-algae-and-green-water-in-your-pond.aspx

Texas A&M AgriLife Extension Service. (n.d.-a). *Rainwater harvesting.* Texas A&M AgriLife Extension Service. https://rainwaterharvesting.tamu.edu/safety/

Texas A&M AgriLife Extension Service. (n.d.-b). *Rainwater harvesting: Above-ground vs belowground.* Texas A&M AgriLife Extension Service. https://rain waterharvesting.tamu.edu/aboveground-vs-belowground/

Texas A&M AgriLife Extension Service. (n.d.-c). *Rainwater harvesting: After-storage treatment.* Texas A&M AgriLife Extension Service. https://rainwa terharvesting.tamu.edu/after-storage-treatment/

Texas A&M AgriLife Extension Service. (n.d.-d). *Rainwater harvesting: Catch-ment Area.* Texas A&M AgriLife Extension Service. https://rainwaterhar vesting.tamu.edu/catchment-area/

Texas A&M AgriLife Extension Service. (n.d.-e). *Rainwater harvesting: Conveyance.* Texas A&M AgriLife Extension Service. https://rainwaterhar vesting.tamu.edu/conveyance/

Texas A&M AgriLife Extension Service. (n.d.-f). *Rainwater harvesting: Fire protection.* Texas A&M AgriLife Extension Service. https://rainwaterhar vesting.tamu.edu/fire-protection/

Texas A&M AgriLife Extension Service. (n.d.-g). *Rainwater harvesting: Land-scaping.* Texas A&M AgriLife Extension Service. https://rainwaterharvest ing.tamu.edu/landscaping/

Texas A&M AgriLife Extension Service. (n.d.-h). *Rainwater harvesting: Livestock.* Texas A&M AgriLife Extension Service. https://rainwaterhar vesting.tamu.edu/livestock/

Texas A&M AgriLife Extension Service. (n.d.-i). *Rainwater harvesting: Pre-*

storage treatment. Texas A&M AgriLife Extension Service. https://rainwa terharvesting.tamu.edu/pre-storage-treatment/

Texas A&M AgriLife Extension Service. (n.d.-j). *Rainwater harvesting: Raingardens.* Texas A&M AgriLife Extension Service. https://rainwaterharvesting. tamu.edu/raingardens/

Texas A&M AgriLife Extension Service. (n.d.-k). *Rainwater harvesting: Roofwater quality.* Texas A&M AgriLife Extension Service. from https:// rainwaterharvesting.tamu.edu/roofwater-quality/

Texas A&M AgriLife Extension Service. (n.d.-l). *Rainwater harvesting: Storage.* Texas A&M AgriLife Extension Service. https://rainwaterharvesting. tamu.edu/storage/

Texas A&M AgriLife Extension Service. (n.d.-m). *Rainwater harvesting: Treatment.* Texas A&M AgriLife Extension Service. https://rainwaterharvesting. tamu.edu/treatment/

Texas A&M AgriLife Extension Service. (n.d.-n). *Rainwater harvesting: Wildlife.* Texas A&M AgriLife Extension Service. https://rainwaterharvesting. tamu.edu/wildlife/

Texas A&M AgriLife Extension Service. (2019a). *Rainwater harvesting: In-home use.* Texas A&M AgriLife Extension Service. https://rainwaterharvesting. tamu.edu/in-home-use/

Texas A&M AgriLife Extension Service. (2019b). *Rainwater harvesting: Rainwater basics.* Texas A&M AgriLife Extension Service. https://rainwaterhar vesting.tamu.edu/rainwater-basics/

Texas A&M AgriLife Extension Service. (2019c). *Rainwater harvesting: Stormwater management.* Texas A&M AgriLife Extension Service. https:// rainwaterharvesting.tamu.edu/stormwater-management/

Texas Water Development Board. (2005). *The Texas manual on rainwater harvesting.* Texas Water Development Board. https://www.twdb.texas.gov/ publications/brochures/conservation/doc/ RainwaterHarvestingManual_3rdedition.pdf

The Renewable Energy Hub USA. (n.d.). *History of rainwater harvesting.* The Renewable Energy Hub. https://www.renewableenergyhub.us/rainwater-harvesting-information/the-history-of-rainwater-harvesting.html

The Watershed. (2013, January 9). *Preparing your rainwater harvesting system for freezing temperatures.* Rain Harvest Systems. https://www.rainharvest.com/ blog/?p=63

Thomas, R. B., Kirisits, M. J., Lye, D. J., & Kinney, K. A. (2014). Rainwater harvesting in the United States: A survey of common system practices. *Journal of Cleaner Production*, *75*, 166–173. https://doi.org/10.1016/j. jclepro.2014.03.073

Thomas, T. H., & Martinson, D. B. (2007). *Roofwater harvesting: A handbook for practitioners*. IRC International Water And Sanitation Centre.

Thompson, M. Y. (2005, March 12). *Passive water harvesting*. New Mexico State University. https://aces.nmsu.edu/ces/yard/2005/031205.html

UBT Digital. (2021, April 19). *Rainwater tank and pump maintenance*. Pumps2You.com. https://pumps2you.com/blogs/news/rainwater-tank-and-pump-maintenance

University of Arizona Cochise County Cooperative Extension Water Wise Program. (2011). Rainwater collection - Calculating water supply and demand to estimate storage needs. In *University of Arizona Cochise County Cooperative Extension*. https://wrrc.arizona.edu/sites/wrrc.arizona.edu/files/UA%20Cochise%20Cty%20Extension_Rainwater%20Collection-%20Calculating%20Water%20Supply%20and%20Demand%20to%20Estimate%20Storage%20Needs.pdf

Vartan, S. (2022, August 16). *A beginner's guide to rainwater harvesting*. Treehugger. https://www.treehugger.com/beginners-guide-to-rainwater-harvesting-5089884

W, J. (2020, November 9). *7 mistakes to avoid when harvesting rain water*. Self-Sufficient Projects. https://selfsufficientprojects.com/7-mistakes-to-avoid-when-harvesting-rain-water/

Waddington, E. (2019, September 21). *Rainwater harvesting system ideas - how to harvest rainwater in your garden*. Happy DIY Home. https://happydiyhome.com/rainwater-harvesting/

Waterfall, P. H. (2004). *Harvesting rainwater for landscape use* (2nd ed.). The University of Arizona College of Agriculture and Life Sciences.

Watson, G. (n.d.). *Rain barrels: A homeowner's guide*. Southwest Florida: Water Management District. https://www.swfwmd.state.fl.us/sites/default/files/store_products/rain_barrels_guide.pdf

Wetec. (n.d.). *Storage tips: How the overflow on a tank works*. Wetec. https://www.wetec.co.za/wetec_why_rainwater/how-the-over%EF%AC%82ow-on-a-tank-works/

Whitworth, R. (2018, May 23). *Safety precautions for rainwater collection*. Blue

and Green Tomorrow. https://blueandgreentomorrow.com/sustainabil
ity/creating-rainwater-collection-system-sustainability/

WIKA Alexander Wiegand. (n.d.). *Level monitoring of grey water and rain water.*
WIKA Alexander Wiegand. https://microsites.wika.com/newscontent
generic_ms.WIKA?AxID=459

Wood, V. (n.d.). *Pump systems for rainwater catchment.* Harvest H2O. https://
www.harvesth2o.com/pump_systems.shtml

IMAGE REFERENCES

AB180. (2017, September 21). *Reflection rain roof texture raining pattern* [Image].
Pixabay. https://pixabay.com/photos/reflection-rain-roof-texture-
2772582/

anaterate. (2018, March 18). *Gabion stones gravel wire frame* [Image]. Pixabay.
https://pixabay.com/photos/gabion-stones-gravel-wire-frame-3235487/

annawaldl. (2017, May 28). *Gooseberry tree watering* [Image]. Pixabay. https://
pixabay.com/photos/gooseberry-tree-watering-2345496/

Brodie. (n.d.). *Water ripples down the side of a fountain photo* [Image]. Burst.
https://burst.shopify.com/photos/water-ripples-down-the-side-of-a-foun
tain?q=overflowing+water

Demidov, A. (2021, November 29). *Flood near palm trees* [Image]. Pexels.
https://www.pexels.com/photo/flood-near-palm-trees-10383330/

Harirak, F. (2022, May 22). *The rain fell on the water, causing the water to splash
into shapes* [Image]. Unsplash. https://unsplash.com/photos/2p-IZO3RIwk

Harrell, L. (2020, September 25). *Algae* [Image]. Unsplash. https://unsplash.
com/photos/yvn5UBRamAM

Ksenia, I. (2021, July 5). *Ripples on puddle* [Image]. Pexels. https://www.pexels.
com/photo/ripples-on-puddle-8605364/

Lane, A. (2020, November 21). *Woman washing fresh fruits in tropical orchard*
[Image]. Pexels. https://www.pexels.com/photo/woman-washing-fresh-
fruits-in-tropical-orchard-5945641/

lenalindell20. (2017, November 12). *Autumn leaf water yellow leaves* [Image].
Pixabay. https://pixabay.com/photos/autumn-leaf-water-yellow-leaves-
2939669/

McMahon, B. (2019, August 2). *An old clay tile roof with moss growing on it* [Image]. Unsplash. https://unsplash.com/photos/WFgOQla6jfQ

Odintsov, R. (2020, October 25). *Close-up photo of groundcover* [Image]. Pexels. https://www.pexels.com/photo/close-up-photo-of-groundcover-5667550/

Pixabay. (2017, August 27). *Fluid pouring in pint glass* [Image]. Pexels. https://www.pexels.com/photo/clean-clear-cold-drink-416528/

Prosa1960. (2015, November 3). *Rain spring roofs* [Image]. Pixabay. https://pixabay.com/photos/rain-spring-roofs-1014194/

ronymichaud. (2014, December 28). *Drop of water* [Image]. Pixabay; Image. https://pixabay.com/photos/drop-of-water-drop-impact-ripples-578897/

Shutterbug75. (2016, March 5). *Background clean connection* [Image]. Pixabay. https://pixabay.com/photos/background-clean-connection-1239373/

Spiske, M. (2018, January 5). *Support yourself - urban gardening - self-supply - self-sufficiency* [Image]. Unsplash. https://unsplash.com/photos/sFydXGrt5OA

Spiske, M. (2020, June 11). *Urban gardening in raised bed - herbs and salad breeding upbringing. Self supply & self-sufficiency* [Image]. Unsplash. https://unsplash.com/photos/bk11wZwb9F4

Wagner, N. (2022, May 27). *Japanese garden, Ashland, Oregon, USA* [Image]. Unsplash. https://unsplash.com/photos/2alyXtTzrlo

www.ingramcontent.com/pod-product-compliance
Lightning Source LLC
Chambersburg PA
CBHW022052020426
42335CB00012B/653